ENCORE

Introductory Lectures on the Western Music Masters

A Classic Collection

For those who value taste.

ENCORE

Introductory Lectures on the Western Music Masters

HANS–JÜRGEN NAGEL

Translated from the German by
SHARMILA BOSE

Original illustrations by
KISHORE CHATTERJEE

SEAGULL BOOKS
CALCUTTA 1987

SEAGULL BOOKS
A Publishing Programme for the
arts and media scene in India

Special xerox effects by M. F. Khan
Cover design by Ashit Paul
ISBN 81 7046 050 6

Published by Naveen Kishore, Seagull Books,
26 Circus Avenue, Calcutta 700 017

Printed in India by T. K. Ray at Journal Printers
50 Sitalatala Lane, Calcutta 700 011

Blocks engraved and printed by Reproduction
Syndicate, 7–1, Bidhan Sarani, Calcutta 700 006

Foreword

The publication of this book coincides with a change in attitude towards Western Classical Music in the Indian sub-continent where the understanding and interpretation of Western music has just begun to take roots the way English studies had done in the last century.

These music lectures had been delivered over a period of two or three years by Hans-Jürgen Nagel, Director of the Max Müller Bhavan, Calcutta, and had come to be known as his Saturday lectures. This book brings together a selection of these, with notes and short musicographies to engage both the beginner and the advanced listener. This book has a practical side and a theoretical, the latter focusing on the musicological gains from social history. There are two depth studies of Symphonies, the Bruckner Eighth and the Mahler Third, Schönberg's favourite symphony. These two articles should kindle further interest in two composers who are fast developing friends in this part of the world. The historically minded will find the two lectures on Schubert and Bruckner particularly relevant, while the lectures on Beethoven's Grosse Fugue, Schumann's Poesy and Electronic music, while touching on fundamentals, also arouse that feeling of curiosity without which a vibrant and continuing enthusiasm for music cannot be sustained.

It must be remembered that these music lectures were originally written out in German. The translator and the editor have deliberately retained some of the original inflections. For style is the man, and these reflections will be treasured as the work of a German musicologist who had tried to widen the audience appeal of Western music in the city by not only opening new doors of perception and establishing better performing standards, but also offering to the non-technical listener a more congenial setting for classical music free from the claustrophobic atmospherics of the conventional concert hall.

KISHORE CHATTERJEE

Preface

Art is understood and presented in a manner very similar to that in which goods are consumed. Understanding is limited to an exchange of facts, data, factors that make the product attractive. But an understanding of art, and especially music, demands more, viz. knowledge of the historical, political and social background of the time and place where the music was born, knowledge of the artist, his aesthetic position, his work as a product of a special historical situation.

This book contains lectures which tried to answer various questions relating to different composers and their music. The lectures were based on the present level of musicological research as presented in the book-series *Musik-Konzepte* edited by H. K. Metzger and Rainer Riehn. I also acknowledge my debt to Constantin Floris' *Bruckner and Brahms* and Frieder Reininghaus' excellent study on music making in the time of Metternich.

Nobody should be prevented from enjoying music and art, and a reading of these lectures could help one to enjoy it more.

H. J. NAGEL

Contents

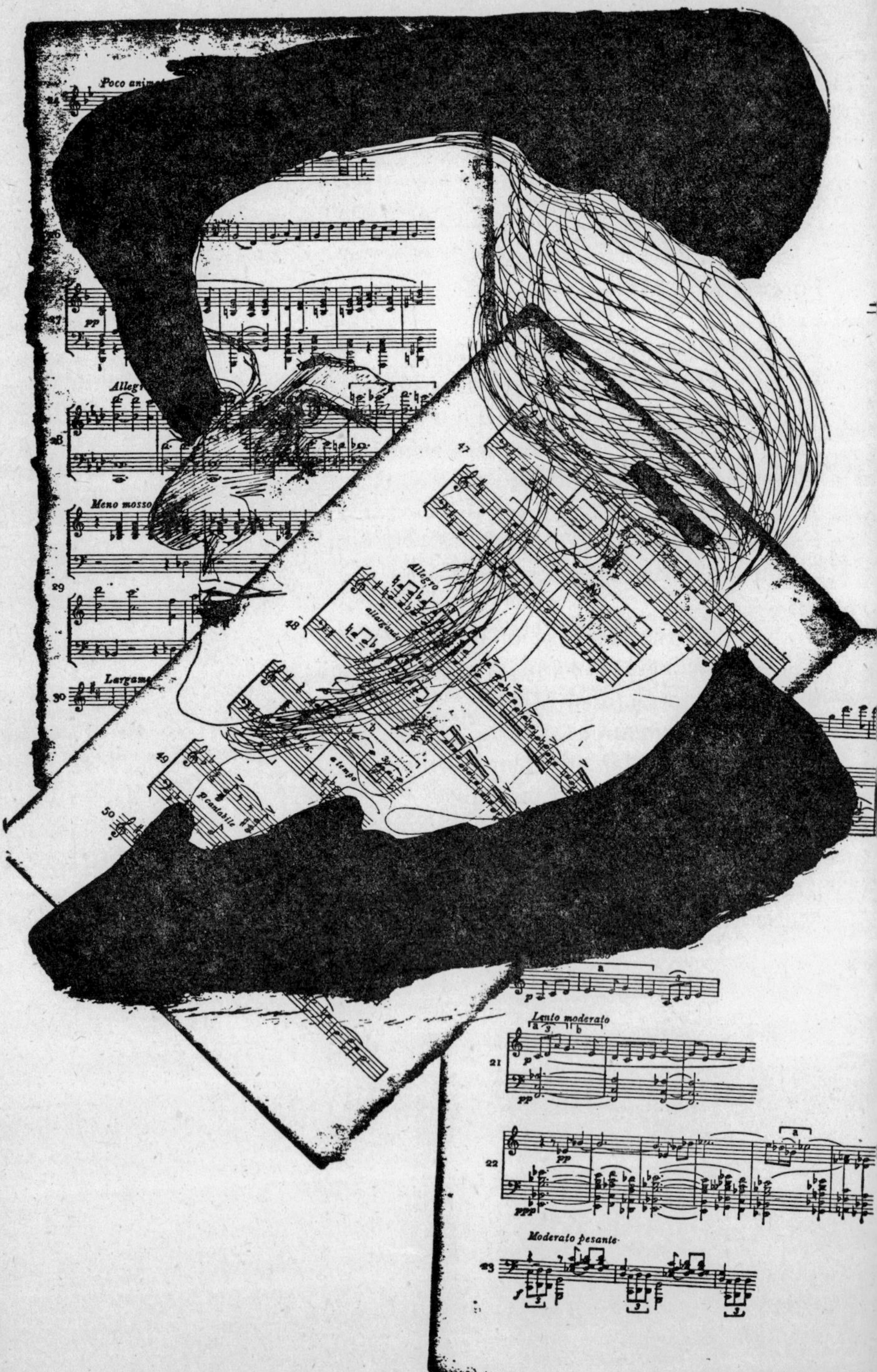

Meno mosso
Allegro
allargando
a tempo
p cantabile
Lento moderato
Moderato pesante

Richard Wagner in British India

In its Eden Gardens the city of Calcutta possesses a beautiful place to serve its—by European standards—highly developed music life. This flower-filled palm park, a promised land of reviving shadows, regularly draws a large mixture of races and nations, one which nowhere else comes closer together as it does under the unifying spell of spiritually and essentially related music. The concerts of the town band do not deprive listeners when it comes to having variety and difficult pieces on the programme—and those who do know about these things, mostly somewhat complacent Europeans, must acknowledge how this native band led by an English conductor masters the difficulties which arise in the intuitive registration of another, albeit related world of sound.

Everywhere, where maharajas or Indian towns have bands of their own, they consist of the basically musical Goanese (natives from Portuguese India—of the land called Goa), and this is true of the band of the Calcutta music centre mentioned earlier, which is of special importance for performances of European and especially German music.

In what does this folk-binding capacity of German music lie? Or to come closer to our topic, where are its points of contact with India? In no case can one speak with authority on the whole subject. Then looking at it from the notion that India would probably lack the least understanding of the modern possibilities of expression, the strict clarity of our classical works would seem to live far out of the way of their perception and sensitivity, as one might be led to conclude from their rejection of modernism.

The space in between the cloud-touching heights of Beethoven and what appears to our ears as the unending monotonal flatness and melodic poverty of Indian music is still too inadequately bridged by efforts made to reach out in the direction of this music-loving people and inform them; and we have the task yet to ensure the further growth and ramification of the branch which has been taken by India from the tree of German music.

With one of our Greats India has forged an unrestrained attachment—to Richard Wagner, whose festive loftiness and vividness in the field of music were indeed totally new to the Indian, yet became understandable in their close dependence on the content of the Opera. Compared with the oft-recurring concept of salvation in the Indian religion, the motifs in *Tannhäuser, Parsifal, The Flying Dutchman* progress on similar lines (compare the essay 'Richard Wagner as a Mystic' by Victor Henkel in the *Deutsche Akademiker Zeitung*), and from this developed the popular and wholehearted branching out into Wagner's complete works.

Whenever Wagnerian music appears on the programme in the Eden Gardens it requires nothing more than a catchy part of *Lohengrin* or *Tannhäuser* to enliven the expressive countenances of the listeners in like proportion to which the drama or the lyrical emotion of the orchestral language increases. And when in one such pleasurable hour the deep pilgrim chorus triumphs over the earthly conjurations of the violins, when the power of the fire magic blazes up high, when the laughter of its flower maidens sounds from the instruments, and the voices of the green stillness rises out of the graphic 'Waldweben' music, then a kinship binding the East with the West also rises in this enigmatic people and we can take pride in that our Bayreuth master also made this string sound.

However, it is not the Goanese band of Eden Gardens alone which brings Wagnerian music to the Indians. In the Empire

Theatre, where indeed till now none of Wagner's Operas have been performed, the Calcutta Military Band of the English Regiments belonging to the stationed garrison plays from his works with almost the same intuitive penetration as similar German organizations would possess.

And even though such performances perhaps hardly find the ideal in the sense of Wagner and the German yardstick, they do not project a false picture, even as they work together with the most heterogeneous mixture of listeners. Wagner in India—that is also an example of how everything weaves itself to a whole, and one in the other lives and moves.

THEODOR RIEBELING,
in *Bayreuther Blätter*, 52nd edition, 1929.

Western Music: Problems of Interpretation

In the development of every music of significance, a fatal stage is eventually reached when the music finally succeeds or 'catches on'. This is the point where it forfeits its revolutionary qualities and becomes neutralized into a cultural 'good' or 'commodity'. The interpretation of the music then aims at finding favour with the listener; and to achieve this end a form of interpretation is found—a form, which is in no way founded upon an analysis of the composition itself. Most of the famous interpreters proceed in their work according to criteria which are very akin to those governing 'light' or 'entertainment' music. By suppressing the compositional structure of the music, in the general run of performances, even Beethoven could one day be turned popular. Music interpreted in this way has a popular appeal, no doubt, but in truth it is a fraud, as it presents the ever subversive world of art as if it had never been designed as a protest against existing reality.

A correct interpretation of music in which its essentially inherent critique of existing society is retained and shown, has of necessity to be non-conformist. The reactions of an average audience, while listening to the works of Beethoven, Schubert and Mozart, as these were performed by the Kolisch Quartet earlier, and as they are played today by the La Salle Quartet, are typical examples of the feeling of alienation which is often experienced when listening to a work being correctly played. It is with displeasure and astonishment that the listener recognizes a feeling of being exposed to a radical composition of the latest date. This phenomenon reveals the great gap which lies between the logical presentation of a work—the product of a diligent analysis of the score—and all the expectations of the music-lovers with their preconceptions of what they seek to cultivate and preserve; the one differs so greatly from the other.

For the correct interpretation of music a few things need to be borne in mind. Attention must be devoted to minute details relating to tempo, to sound-dynamics, i.e. the right volume, to logical phrasing and expression, and finally, though no less important, to clear intonation. Accurate interpretation of music always functions as a negation of the established and dominating culture. This is especially true of Beethoven's music. The conductor Gustav Mahler was the first musician to introduce this logical negation in his work. This new way of performing was called 'gegen den Strich musizieren', a phrase which translates as 'against the traditional or prevalent way of making music'. With his novel performances he destroyed every false consensus in the accepted way of playing even such popular symphonies as the Fifth. Mahler's attitude towards tradition is crystallized in his oft-quoted words—'what you call tradition is nothing other than your convenience and slovenliness'. In an attempt to qualify a 'performance', Rudolf Kolisch has defined it as the 'Realization of the Musical Sense', in his book of the same name.

As recognized interpreters of Beethoven it is generally acknowledged that after the Kolisch Quartet it is only the La Salle Quartet, based in Cincinnatti, Ohio, that possesses the ability to play Beethoven's Chamber Music as it should be played. The technical and theoretical problems which are confronted while playing his music had actually been solved long ago. On 29 December 1942, before the Congress of the American Musicological Society, Kolisch gave a lecture on 'Tempo and Character in Beethoven's Music'. It is not possible to play Beethoven meaningfully to any extent, if one is not acquainted with Kolisch's research in this field.

Kolisch reconstructed the authentic Beethoven tempi. Going by the few pieces that Beethoven had metronomized himself, and using them as a base, it is possible to establish every tempo without ambiguity. This can be done by drawing an analogy between the verbal tempo description and the individual musical character, in which every element in Beethoven's music is distinctly countable. The Beethoven tempi reconstructed by Kolisch are, as a rule, quicker than the usual inaccurate ones. The advantages of this are many. Not only does it change the proportions in the music by tautening it, but features of purely sensational moods such as pathos, 'the festive', 'the ceremonial'—features which the listener normally grows to expect as 'positive value'—are also eliminated, as are the mistakes in the phrasing and in dynamics. Provocatively expressed, it may be said that the bourgeois society, which itself at one time was a revolutionary one, can no longer afford an honest interpretation of its music. This society cannot face a music in which there is inherent a negation of its complacency. As a consequence of this the culture business aims at making the music 'enjoyable'. It seeks to neutralize the intellect, the nature of the intellect being to question the existing and to search for its negation. Proof of the commercial society's desire to imbue the intellect with the mentality of mindless consumption, was to be seen quite early in the trend of naming confectionery as 'Leibnizkeks', 'Schillerlocken', and 'Mozartkugeln'.

Poco animato
Più mosso
Moderato maestoso
Allegro
Meno mosso
Moderato pesante

The Morality of *The Magic Flute*

The Magic Flute is at the same time one of the most united and disunited German operas. Its many-levelled structure is surrounded by numerous speculations and interpretations of musical research. Mythology, Freemasonry, social criticism and Enlightenment are concepts which repeatedly pose problems for the producer who thinks of staging *The Magic Flute.* Another problem is the historical background in the person of the librettist, Emmanuel Schikaneder, who, shrewd as he was, knew what was and what was not possible in the Vienna of 1790. Magical and mechanical comedies, where so many illusions could be conjured up on the stage, were popular. But not all magical titles were as successful as Mozart's *The Magic Flute.*

Eternal, valid for all times and all peoples, *The Magic Flute* is inextricably bound up with the petty ambition of a poet deliberately seeking the popular approval of a suburban Viennese public. One needs an explanatory and intermediary historical criticism to understand and do justice to the whole work in its randomly created uniqueness. If we juxtapose the different elements of this work, we come upon a speaking proof of the tragedy in the destiny of a creative mind forced to submit in its working to the conditions of time and place. A suburban Viennese theatre with a theatre director speculating in the taste of his public delivers the greatest musician of his time with a text for an effect piece to save himself from bankruptcy by this collaboration. Mozart writes for this text music of eternal beauty. But this beauty is inseparably embodied in the work of this theatre director, and, in reality, remains rooted in this indissoluble connection, understandable in its original form to only the Viennese public. In an unaffected way, *The Magic Flute* communicated completely at the level of their own taste of that time. If we hope to judge and understand *The Magic Flute* completely we must be able—by some modern spiritist magic—to imagine ourselves in the Viennese theatre in the year of its first staging. Would a modern production of the Berlin Court Theatre give us the same understanding?

Mozart sees music as ideology created by man, in which each 'direction' is a 'placing'. In 1791 he was confronted with ruins, the ruin of his composition (and of his life) and the ruin of society. Art had fallen apart, the division of labour had taken its toll. In this moment of disintegration, the spheres of 'higher' and 'lower' music were juxtaposed, adjacent but not integrated, for the first and last time, as though this situation was perfectly natural. Immediately afterwards this was not possible any more. Today's music also labours in vain to bridge this chasm. Adorno writes: 'Haydn, the Mozart of *The Magic Flute* and Beethoven are completely unimaginable without the interaction between the two already separated spheres. The last time they came together on a narrow ridge was in Mozart's *The Magic Flute;* characters like Strauss' and Hofmannsthal's Ariadne look back to this moment with sorrowful longing. Till late into the nineteenth century it was possible to have light music with decorum. This phase of its aesthetic decline is coupled with an irrevocable dis-association of these two spheres. As Nietszche said, "The good old times are over, in Mozart they sang their last song . . ." '[1]

Enlightenment in the theatre was not the abstract Enlightenment of literature, and could therefore appear publicly in an oriental disguise—*Isis and Osiris,* just as they appear right next to nursery rhymes, step out of the brightest sphere of Enlightenment into this magic setting of humanitarianism. Not only Enlightenment but its most productive product, the revolution, hung in the air, or, rather, was already under way. Fairy tale characters, Egyptomania (years before Napoleon marched into Egypt, before Champollion's deciphering of the hieroglyphs) and Freemasonry were ideal disguises and masks for the opera, behind which the real ideas of the time were hidden to pass them through censorship. Of course later on, after the death of Joseph II, Freemasonry, which was allied to Jacobinism and had become synonymous with the hated social progress, was banned. The opera lay under suspicion, doubts had arisen, the anonymous author of a paper entitled 'The Secret Response of the Conspiratorial Methods of Jacobins in the Austrian States', writes, 'The idea which lies at the bottom of this piece is: freeing the French people from old despotism through the wisdom of new laws.'

The underlying maxims of *The Magic Flute*—reason, virtue, justice, tolerance, nature—do not exclude such interpretations. Sarastro is the anti-despot; Tamino, who is destined to be his successor, is a 'prince' in the same sense as Rousseau's 'sovereign' in the *Contrat Social*; the ruler himself is the people. This does not contradict the theocratic reign of Sarastro, as Voltaire's verdict against religion was applicable neither to Rousseau, a non-atheist, nor to the French Revolution, which was influenced by him in its determining phases. Rousseau's *Contrat Social* ends with a chapter entitled 'On the Civil Religion', whose 'religious laws should be simple, few in number, precisely expressed without explanations or commentaries.' They consist in 'the recognition of a Divinity which is all-powerful, wise, beneficent, foresighted and provident', they proclaim 'a future life, punishment of the bad and rewarding of the good', they include 'the holiness of the social contracts and laws'. Besides the 'positive and infallible dogmas', there are also the negative religious dogmas, which are restricted to one law, 'intolerance', which is 'part of all the cults which have been expelled by us'. This means that 'one must tolerate every religion which tolerates others, as long as their religious laws do not contradict the duties of the citizen. Whoever dares to state, "There is no salvation outside of the church", must be exiled from the State, unless the State is the Church and the ruler the high priest.' The same applies to Sarastro's kingdom.

The little which remained of the original progressive ideas of Freemasonry was, at least in Austria and South Germany, already dead and buried by 1790. In the Lodges, which rather resembled Rotary Clubs, the aristocrats set the tone: Rosicrucians, Jesuits, anyone who had a protected status was admitted. Even during the reign of the supposedly liberal Joseph II, those Lodge brothers who were also members of the more progressive Illuminati Order were persecuted by the State. No one dared to express any liberal thoughts. Under such circumstances, how many fruitful ideas could possibly be preserved in *The Magic Flute*?

The symbols of the bird and the bird-catcher also have a direct connection with the symbolism of Freemasonry, also with the women's Lodges, known as 'adoption Lodges'. Why is a bird-catcher used? The answer is to be found in the rituals of the adoption Lodges: a living bird was used as an image to warn against feminine curiosity, and in this way the bird becomes a symbol of the 'fair sex'. Now one can understand why Papageno sells his birds to the ladies for the use of the Queen of the Night, and why he is given food and livelihood by them in return. The symbol is not a gallant one, but none the less transparent.

1 Theodor W. Adorno, *Versuch über Wagner*, München 1964.

388
Moderato
Moderato pesante

Fidelio 1806

'Beethoven's opera *Fidelio,* newly revised, was performed at the Theatre an der Wien. The revision consists of the condensation of three Acts into two. It is incomprehensible how the composer could bring himself to enliven this trivial and worthless work by Sonnleithner with the beautiful music. For—not counting the lowly intrigues by reputable persons—the effect of the whole cannot possibly be of the kind that the musician had intended, because the senselessness of the recited parts, wholly or to a great extent wipes out the beautiful impression made by the singing parts. Mr Beethoven is certainly not lacking in a high aesthetic understanding of his Art, because he knows how to express the sentiment lying in the words that he has to handle, excellently, but he appears to be failing in the capacity to take an overall view and to evaluate the text with regard to the total effect. The music is indeed masterly, and Beethoven demonsrates what he is capable of producing in the future in this new direction that he has taken.

'The first duet and both the quartets are especially pleasing. In contrast to this however, the overture fails to do so, due to the incessant dissonance and to the overloaded, almost non-stop humming of the violins. It is more an artificial artistry than real Art.

'Mlle Müller, as a disguised Fidelio, sings the—for her charming, although little trained voice—exactly calculated part very well; only she cannot free herself from the embrace of her rescued husband at the end. Also Mlle Müller, well beloved for her erstwhile extremely beautiful figure, did her best.'

That was from a review in *Zeitung für die elegante Welt* (No. 56, 10 May 1806, Spalte 455) of *Fidelio*, after the première of the second version on 29 March 1806.

Fidelio was performed only once more on 10 April 1806. The reason why it was withdrawn so quickly although public response was not lacking, was Beethoven's obstinacy. He felt himself discriminated against financially. Because he got a percentage of the net profits of a performance, he demanded to look at the accounts. When Baron Braun, the director of Theater an der Wien at the time, showed him the cash receipts, with the information that on both evenings, the house was only partially occupied and that too in the less expensive seats, Beethoven answered brusquely, in his habitual uncompromising manner, that he did not write for the galleries. The discussion became more heated and ended with Beethoven categorically recalling his scores. With this the history of the *Fidelio* performances came to an end for the time being.

As singular as the opera *Fidelio* itself, is the fact that Beethoven wrote four overtures for it. The first of them was never played at any of the performances. This is why it did not appear in print before the year 1838. After a private trial performance of the so-called First *Leonore* overture (Op. 138) in the house of the Count Lichnowsky, Beethoven was convinced that the problem of the opera overture had not been solved satisfactorily with this piece because it did not have the desired effect on the audience. For the performances of the first two versions of the opera, he created two versions of another overture—the *Leonore* overture nos. 2 and 3. While the latter version was already published in 1810, the earlier alternative version was not printed before 1842.

For the third version of *Fidelio,* Beethoven wrote an absolutely different overture. In this version, for the first time, the A major duet between Marzelline and Jaquino begins the opera; as a result the major of the first three overtures had to give way to a new key—the E major.

On 11 January 1840, Felix Mendelssohn Bartholdy conducted all the four overtures together for the first time, one after the other in a concert in the Leipziger Gewandhaus. Robert Schumann wrote enthusiastically about the performance in the *Neuen Zeitschrifte für Musik* (The New Music Magazine), founded and edited by Schumann from 1833:

What the Leipzig Orchestra performed on last Thursday should be printed in golden letters—'All four overtures to *Fidelio*—one after the other'. Thanks be to the Viennese of 1805 that the first did not appeal to them, so that Beethoven in a godly wrath created one overture after the other. If he had never appeared colossal to me before, it was so that we could behold him at work that evening. We saw him better than ever before in his workshop—constructing, rejecting, changing—always glowing and hot. He appeared perhaps most gigantic in his second approach. The first overture would not please you, he thought. In the second, you will forget to think, he thought, and went to work anew, letting the touching drama overwhelm him and make him sing of the great suffering and joy of his lovers, once more.

The Dramaturgy of *Fidelio*

Beethoven's only opera has always been criticized as being athwart to the genre in as much as in the first version (*Leonore*, 1805) it surrendered to the urge for symphonic breadth found in most of Beethoven's music. The *Eroica* with its great dimensions had already been composed in 1803. This symphonic element, it has always been felt, runs contrary to, or at least highly endangers, the vital dramatic nerve of the stage plot. However faulty the objection may be, it is one that is difficult to refute. If Beethoven's unique opera is considered from the standpoint of the aesthetic values associated with Mozart's operas —aesthetic values that were but short-lived in history—then Mozart's universal presentation of life-like human beings may well be said to triumph over the figures in the wretched, cliché-filled libretto that Sonnleithner and then Treitschke (1814) worked up for Beethoven from Bouilly's French drama. But in saying this we do not take into consideration Beethoven's entirely different musical and dramatic aims. His conception of the purpose of art—with its self-imposed social duty, to use today's terms—differs in its essence from the conception of Mozart. Beethoven was the first composer in the history of music to set up his music as a moral authority and as a political conscience. These particular features necessarily encumbered his new aesthetic rigour while Mozart in his great operas captured, for the last time before the bourgeois revolution, the homogeneous, completely unified and highly differentiated picture of the people of his days in a way that can never again be repeated. Beethoven, on the other hand, appeals, admonishes, threatens, despairs and draws up, in the words of Ernst Bloch, 'wish-filled pictures of the moment of fulfilment' in his music, whether instrumental or vocal. He shared with Mozart and Haydn the idea that music has a characteristic language that does not necessarily need words. As Bloch says, 'It is and will remain the fate of even the good text, even of the estimable poetic text, even of the musically most completely incorporated text, to become in the final analysis the beggar in the face of the musical tones. Leonore and Florestan sing, "O nameless joy"; even at its simplest and rawest levels the music quietly overcomes the words and makes them its reflection'.[1] But Beethoven was the first to discover the 'charged' tone. His music in itself contains dramatic action, complete developments, achieved goals. It is, therefore, no exaggeration to say that Beethoven did not seek an operatic story, but rather that his music found its dramatic realization in the theatre —even if it was on the stage of shallow melodrama.

It is easy to put one's finger on the weak points of the libretto: the embarrassing and improbable 'trouser role' of Leonore that, unlike the operatic convention of the eighteenth century, is treated as a temporary disguise, not as a type of role. Then again, the fact that Marzelline rejects Jaquino's proposal of marriage because she has unwittingly fallen in love with the supposedly male Fidelio borders upon the ridiculous. Yet, the disguise, indeed, the fraudulent deceit, is dramatically an indispensable means to enable Leonore to achieve her real goal. The 'bourgeois family play with its false bottom', is the way Harry Goldschmidt characterizes the 'Singspiel' level of the opera, thus projecting it as the springboard for Leonore's scheme to enter the Keeper's living quarters—even at the risk of having to accede to the world of his narrow-minded life and ideas, in order to gain access to the prisoners (to Florestan) and to carry out her rescue plan. She turns her back on Jaquino's ridiculous scenes of jealousy, Marzelline's despondent 'happy-home' notions of married life (that make one rather sad) and Rocco's opportunistic zeal in duty (that is rather suspicious). The actions of the villain Pizarro also bear melodramatic features, as well as Florestan's visions of angels and of rescue and, above all, the rending tension in the dungeon scene with its drawn dagger, pistol, noble display of courage and the 'signal' of the trumpet.

Treitschke brought all of these elements into a consistently linear development of the plot for the final version of the opera, that, unlike the first version, steered towards the gigantic antiphonary 'colon' of the trumpet signal without interruption or diversion, not letting the audience catch its breath until the subsequent last Finale. There is a spiral ascent through the various levels of what can be termed the 'hope principle'. First comes the Singspiel with its limited hope for 'little' people. Then grand opera with its basic comprehension of love and freedom as moral categories that do not simply exist but must be won. Lastly oratorio, the statuary scene as a 'wishful thinker's picture of the moment of fulfilment', the utopian interlacing of love with freedom and freedom with love. As demanded by ethical severity, the characters grow beyond their empirically comprehensible existence to develop into the embodiment of ideas; for example, Leonore, whose original and personal intention was to free her own husband, upon seeing the misery in the dungeon, transforms her concern from the level of personal love for her husband into that of basic moral insight, into a super-personal feeling for humanity: 'Whoever you are, I'll save you'. Thus in the end there is liberation of the oppressed in general.

1 Ernst Bloch, *Zur Philosophie der Neuen Musik,* Frankfurt 1974.

The Great Controversy over the *Grosse Fugue*

The manuscript of the fugue, which originally formed the final movement of the Quartet, Op. 130, and was called an 'Overture', can be found in the music department of the Berlin State Library (Artaria collection). The first edition, which appeared in May 1827, a few days after Beethoven's death, bears the following title:

> 'Grand Fugue, free and artificial for two Violins, Alto and Violoncello. Dedicated with the deepest respect to His Imperial Highness the most Eminent Cardinal Rudolph, Archduke of Austria, Prince of Hungary and Bohemia, Archbishop of Ollmütz, etc. Grand Cross of the Hungarian Order of St. Etienne etc. etc. by L. van Beethoven, Op. 133. Property of the Publisher Math. Artaria, Vienna.'

The right to publish the Quartet in B flat major, Op. 130, which Beethoven had first offered to Schlesinger in July 1825, was usurped by the Viennese art and music dealer, Matthias Artaria. On 9 January 1826, he paid Beethoven the agreed fee of 80 ducats for the manuscript. The engraving of the score was ready by the middle of August 1826. 'Artaria', Karl Holz recalled more than thirty years later in a letter written to Wilhelm von Lenz on 16 July 1857, 'now gave me the extremely delicate task of persuading Beethoven to replace the Fugue—so difficult to comprehend—by another concluding piece which would be easier both for the performers and for the public to understand. I put it to Beethoven that the Fugue was a work of art outside the sphere of normal string quartet compositions, and even outside his newest, unconventional quartets, bidding that it should stand alone, with an opus number of its own. Artaria was quite willing to pay an extra fee for a new finale. Beethoven asked for time to consider the matter, but on the very next day I received a letter in which he declared himself willing to do as had been requested.'[1] Beethoven however did not decide all that quickly to make this radical change in his work which Artaria wanted. The second finale was not written until some time between September and November 1826. Beethoven sent it to Haslinger on 11 November with the request that he should hand it over to Artaria 'only against the payment of 15 ducats in gold.' In May 1827 Artaria published the Quartet in B flat major with the second finale as Op. 130 (dedication to Galitzin) and also—as a separate work—the Great Fugue with the opus number 133 and a dedication to the Cardinal Archduke Rudolph of Austria (both in score and parts).

So much for the history of the composition. The question as to why Beethoven agreed to separate the Great Fugue from the Quartet in B flat, and compose a new finale to replace it, has led to highly contradictory speculations by writers on Beethoven. Mahaim,[2] in his book, pleads for the original version (as various distinguished musicologists and quartet players have done before him). He attempts to reconstruct the course of events in 1826 accurately, and to account for them psychologically. Admittedly his interpretation, despite the documentary evidence he has assembled in support, and convincing though it appears, cannot settle the question beyond all doubt. It is, however, certain that Beethoven did not willingly and immediately agree to the 'mutilation' (Romain Rolland) of his Quartet in B flat. This is borne out by another statement of Karl Holz (in a letter to Otto Jahn in October 1852, which contradicts his later statement to Wilhelm von Lenz in 1857, already quoted): 'He held it (the Great Fugue) in high regard, and was only persuaded with difficulty to separate it from the Quartet'.[3] Entries in the conversation-books which Beethoven used early in 1826 prove that Artaria and Holz pleaded with him several times for the Fugue to be published separately—first on 11 April, three weeks after the unsuccessful first performance of the original version of Op. 130. During that month of April, Artaria had made a piano arrangement of the Fugue for four hands. The arranger was the pianist Anton Haim, but Beethoven did not approve of it. In August, after his nephew's attempted suicide, which came as a terrible shock to him, and after completing the Quartet in C sharp minor, Beethoven himself made a transcription for four hands of the

Great Fugue. As Artaria attached great importance to the separate publication of this piano version, he accepted the new arrangement, and on September paid the fee of 12 ducats that Beethoven had asked for. (This version was also published in May 1827, as Op. 134). Not until then, i.e. nearly five months after Artaria's first intervention, had Beethoven agreed to compose a new finale for Op. 130.

Mahaim's thesis is that the removal of the Great Fugue from its context as part of the Quartet in B flat took place in two stages, in a roundabout way and contrary to Beethoven's wishes. First, there was the separation of the Fugue, prompted by the making of the two four-hand piano transcriptions—an almost 'Machiavellian step'; then replacement of the Fugue by the Rondo Finale, totally different in character. The fact that Beethoven allowed himself to be persuaded to destroy the organic structure of his work is all the more astonishing in view of his earlier rejection of requests to make alterations of far lesser importance. For example, on 19 February 1813, he replied to the publisher Thomson in Edinburg, who had asked Beethoven to make changes in nine of his Scottish folk songs, with a categorical refusal (originally in French): 'I am not accustomed to retouching my compositions. I have never done so, as I am convinced of the fact that even a partial alteration changes the character of the composition.' At that time, Beethoven preferred to compose the Scottish songs anew, rather than make alterations in the existing pieces. Making a radical change in one of his last great works must have been far more repugnant to him. Since existing documents do not provide a clear solution to this problem, the best that can be done here is probably to draw attention to the very poor state of Beethoven's health, both physical and psychological, during the autumn of 1826, which may well have resulted in the fact that his artistic and moral powers were no longer sufficiently strong to resist the pressure put on him to make the change. Was this the despairing action of a sick and broken man? An element of uncertainty remains, and it is difficult to give a categorical 'yes' or 'no' to that question.

1 W. von Lenz, *Beethoven: eine Kunststudie*, vol. 4, Hamburg 1860.
2 Ivan Mahaim, *Beethoven: Naissance et Renaissance des Derniers Quatuors*, Paris 1964.
3 Friedrich Kerst, *Die Erinnerungen an Beethoven*, vol. 2, Stuttgart 1913.

Poco animato
388
Allegro
a tempo
allarg.
a tempo
Più mosso
Moderato pesante

Franz Schubert

Franz Schubert lived in an era of Restoration. When he was born in Vienna in 1797 the Jacobin trials were just coming to an end. Sections of the people who had shown themselves to be on the side of the French Revolution were now being brought once again under the yoke of the feudal order with imprisonment and executions meant to serve as deterrent examples. The intelligentsia faced intimidation. Among the intellectuals the reform ideas of Joseph II were far more widespread than ideas more radically revolutionary. The Jacobin trials were in fact 'Josephin-trials'. Franz II (1792–1835) wanted to retain and preserve the good old conditions by using all possible means including that of terror.

Schubert came from the dark shadows of the Vienna suburbs. For thirty-two years of his life he was under the pressure of Restoration conditions. His upbringing in the pious and loyal household of an elementary schoolteacher, his institutional training as a royal court choir boy under the church, the distinctively petit-bourgeois forms of thinking and living in his immediate surroundings, the pressures of a capitalistic music-market, the development of which had just got under way, the arduous and unhygienic living conditions in the Viennese suburbs, and finally —very decisively—the pressure of the Metternichian system and of police-commissioner Sedlnitzky affect his life. Schubert's talent as a composer surfaced explosively in the years of the German and Austrian war of liberation against the alien Napoleonic domination. In 1813–14 alone about three hundred new pieces were written. The brief enthusiasm for liberty in those stormy years was clearly reflected in the enthusiastic speed of Schubert's production, just as a depressive and wistful mood was reflected in his earlier series of complaining, mournful songs, with which his work as a composer had begun. In 1815 the stir and bustle of the Vienna Congress had crossed its peak. The eighteen year old teaching-assistant set to music yet another series of freedom songs on texts by Theodor Körner on the year 1813.

But the days of bourgeois high spirits soon came to an end. The call for freedom, now also raised by the native counts and aristocrats, would soon come under repression. Naturally the 'great subject' of the infamous 'Karlsbad Resolution' of 1819 was still discussed within the closed circles of friends, in intellectual gatherings, only at the still legal meeting-points, the special inns and coffee-houses. But reticence and restraint were imperative in public or semi-public utterances, including the messages expressed in art. Language and pictures soon came to be coded.

The idea of an Escape from Reality is indisputably present in Schubert's work. He rediscovered himself in his circle of friends with his Schubertiades and in the reality of merry and jovial tavern-evenings.

But Schubert's music is not merely an ecstatic escape into a better world. Although from the start it had something of this function, unlike much of the poetry stemming from the circle of his friends, his music allows for intrusions of reality, and develops dream-pictures and realistic moments. As is true of life which apparently seems to progress on well-ordered tracks, his music also includes anarchistic features. Alongside the struggle to reach to a social standard of 'Form', there are elements of rejection and refusal, of protest against the conservatives, of subtle provocation, of cheeky parody, of the vassal's insubordination and of a simple demonstration of musical freedom. At the same time—and this ought not to be overlooked by the leftist critics of Schubert—from the start to the finish his music combines and binds many things with Austrian folk music.

Schubert's music 'speaks' of freedom and 'dreams' of freedom. The fact that his music does not speak more and concretely about freedom should be viewed against the background of the other fact that hardly anyone of the staunch and steadfast social revolutionaries in the main years of Schubert's creativity agitated openly and candidly for the collapse of Feudal Absolutism; and if someone did it he was speedily silenced, intimidated, imprisoned or forced into exile. One can of course criticize Schubert, the suburban musician, for not having become a martyr. No artist can rise so easily above the limitations of the times in which he lives; to demand this of him or to contend this would mean to encourage a belief in the 'cult of genius'.

At Himmelpfortgrund in 1786 Franz Theodore Schubert took charge of the school which had somewhat gone to pot—a school with barely two dozen children. The Himmelpfort school was housed in two rooms of the house 'Zum rothen Krebs'—the Schubert-House which still stands on the Nussdorferstrasse. It provided accommodation to sixteen parties including the landlord, each had a room with a kitchen. In the kitchenette was born Franz Schubert, the twelfth child to be born to his parents, and even if only five of them survived—four brothers and a sister—it is incomprehensible by modern standards how the affairs of the school and the family could be conducted with any regularity, within the cramped space of four rooms and the dire poverty.

Father Schubert—righteous, upright, hardworking—was also a good-natured man. In a few years the number of his scholars had grown to 200, and he was forced to seek larger quarters and was unable to manage any more without assistants. No matter how poor one was in Lichtenthal and in Himmelpfortgrund, it was by no means a poor locality. The old Viennese song sung by the washer-folk of Himmelpfortgrund—who in all the work of their days could 'feel sadness well'—reveals that they knew sadness very well—and it reflects the spirit of the people among whom Franz Schubert grew up. It was a world by itself—away from the city and yet within its sheltering protection—in which with all the narrowness one also had the broad wideness of Nature. There were the father and the brothers with whom one could play quartets from scores that had been cleanly copied by hand; and there was the parish church where a choir taught one the basic elements of counterpoint.

The father—Franz Theodore, living far out in Lichtenthal, simply called 'the meadow' by the people, a teacher in a school—was a resolute and determined man. All his sons were capable, especially Franz. And so he himself put Franz into a seminary in the city. But in difficult times, which were not spared him as the youth began to grow into a man, he would often think whether he would not have done better to have left the boy in Lichtenthal.

Conflicts between the larger and the smaller world

The conflict between the larger and the smaller world was thus to become the theme of the life of this schoolteacher's son—and unavoidably also that of his parental home. And if on occasions there were bitter quarrels between father and son, they still managed to hold on to each other valiantly; they even found a base and paid for the shafts of lightning which struck because the son of the Lichtenthal schoolmaster was a genius. For, one must not forget that after completing his period at the seminary—out in Säulengasse—while he was his father's assistant at school, Schubert composed over one-third of his works—among them symphonies, operas, masses. It will never be possible to find out how this was possible purely from the point of view of time. The circumstances in which he achieved this have been described by Louis Schlösser, a violinist who had temporarily lived with father Schubert as a sub-tenant before the family moved to the almost luxurious conditions of the newly constructed school-building in Rossau: 'As I visited him in his flat in the suburb Rossau, it was known to me that Schubert did not live in excellent conditions and yet the total absence of every comfort astonished me. In a spacious room on ground level which looked more like the workshop of a craftsman than the study of a composer, I saw a piano crowded with notebooks for writing scores; string instruments, music stands, the necessary chairs and stools in disorder and otherwise not a trace of comfort was to be seen—this was the home of the young master of art, the place from where such rich treasures of overflowing fullness of emotions came.

For his father and his brothers it was a great pleasure to play together with him in a quartet. This happened mostly during vacations. The youngest was the most sensitive among them all. If a mistake was made anywhere—no matter how small—Franz would look at the culprit either earnestly or with a smile on his face.

The Magic Flute : Papageno, as Schikaneder performed him, 1791.

The Magic Flute : Papageno, as Oskar Kokoschka conceived him, 1965.

Schumann and Clara Wieck.

Wagner, the evening before his death : in a drawing by Paul von Joukowsky.

A Turning Point

For Schubert's father and brothers the glowing enthusiasm with which he made music was a familiar sight—on which they looked with complacent pride, rather than wasting too many words on it. Friends of the Schuberts such as Josef von Spaun were sooner struck by the almost trembling excitement with which the boy—and later the youth—surrendered himself to music. Purely technically, Schubert was perhaps better on the violin; but his piano-playing excited deeper sensation. In his approach to the piano, first there was the natural curiosity about technical matters which is hidden in every boy as it shows itself in a piano-maker's workshop; but there was another aspect, a far more astonishing independence in making the mechanism of the instrument subservient to himself.

His brother Ignaz wrote, 'I was very surprised when after a few months he informed me that he did not require any further lessons from me and that he was going to teach himself in future. In reality he progressed so far in a short time that I myself had to recognize him as a master far surpassing me and one I could never catch up with.'

Schubert, who never became a real pianist (nor did he want to be one), soon proved himself to be an extraordinarily suggestive pianist, suggestive for others as well as for himself; for his early piano works show, in their series of continually occurring new ideas, how greatly this instrument lured him to pure endless fantasy. They also show however that he found it easier to express himself on the keyboard than to find his way into the Form, which alone ultimately decides the value or the worthlessness of the richest streams of thoughts.

The piano sonata in A minor was composed towards the end of 1823 at yet another turning point in Schubert's life. The entry into the great Form with his personal form is unmistakably consummated. But at the same time the fatal disease which attacked him proved to be a grave turning point in his life after which life with the family and with his friends could not go on in the way it had up to then. Schubert alone did not suffer terribly; for his father too, who had in the meantime become the principal of a much larger school in Rossau and who was soon to receive

Viennese citizen-rights, the affair must have been a terrible one.

Whoever listens to the A minor sonata can decide for himself whether he can see in it a mirrored reflection of the great conflicts which were beginning to build up before him. One should not lose oneself too much in the area of the descriptive in this wonderful piece. Schubert had not written any piano sonatas for over three years before he wrote this work in which thoughtful reflection is combined with great climaxes and spacious development. The sound levels in the flowing first movement, the mastery in the precise recolouring at the markedly reminiscent Slavic moments allow the sonata to step out of the limitations of its very private context. Here Schubert stands before us in his totality.

In the heights of the Absolute

That life could not remain for Schubert the way it had been in Lichtenthal was clear. To find a combination of parental home and friendship might have been possible for a talent but not for a genius. His circle of friends were drawn with irresistible power into a world which was closed even to most of these young people; a world the existence of which at the best only some could guess at. Schubert also had to experience the good and easy times—like his first day in the Hungarian Schloss Zselitz—where things went wonderfully well with him, but were for a person like him not the most productive period. The release and freedom from trouble has never been good for a genius. It is good for talents. Genius needs anguish, tribulation and difficulty, through which it can be released, redeemed and unleashed. When Schubert came to Hungary the second time he was already sick. At that time he wrote his brother Ferdinand a letter which is often misinterpreted. Ferdinand had reported that they were once again playing quartets at his house and—perhaps to please him—also mentioned that Franz's quartets too were part of them. Besides he took care to go once a week to the guest-house 'Zur ungarischen Krone' to listen to the musical box there playing Franz's waltzes. To this Schubert answered, 'But it would be better if you would restrict yourself to quartets other than mine, for there is nothing in it except the fact that they please you—

you who are fond of everything that comes from me. Your remembering me and thinking of me would be better so especially as they do not appear to move you as much as the waltzes at the "Ungarische Krone".' Schubert's observation, behind which were perhaps thoughts of the late Haydn's quartets and Mozart and Beethoven quartets, have been interpreted as a sign of too much modesty. Not as if Schubert was immodest. But he had in the meantime come to realize that the understanding of the real essence could only begin beyond such youthful memories, and therefore wanted to prevent his much-loved brother from missing out on the view which lay beyond the fence of faithful devotion. The posthumously found Quartet movement in C-minor written in 1820 stands on the border. Theresé Grob was lost, the separation from his friend Mayrhofer was in the offing. Schubert stood there where he apparently belonged always, namely, alone. It did not need the catastrophe of his illness to bring this home to him. Neither was this realization made more manifest by his separation from the great, convivial, stimulating and yet again—for it could not have been otherwise—unbinding circle of the Schubertians.

The music has something vibrating, something haunted, specially in its return to quietude, to bliss, an uncommonly agile slenderness. It has been claimed that this C-minor movement had been privately performed, but this is very doubtful. Ferdinand's house quartét was anyhow, according to a description his brother Ignaz wrote to Zselitz, not up to the standard: 'That for some time now I have been an honorary member of a small music society you already know. Only I must tell you that these musical evening entertainments may—not wholly incorrectly—be compared to a horse-drawn vehicle, which often turns over and which without a competent driver is very difficult to bring into motion again'.

The three worlds had separated from one another a long time ago, for such a quartet movement ventures into the heights of the absolute where the air is too thin and rarefied for the family and for the best of friends.

385
Poco animato
Più mosso
388
Moderato
Moderato pesante

Schumann's Musical Poesy

An examination of the assessment of Robert Schumann in the music literature of the nineteenth century reveals a significant discrepancy. Before 1850, Schumann was numbered among the progressive composers of his time, and after 1850 the 'Neudeutschen' classified him as a conservative. The witticism that Schumann was a genius who had ended as a talent, originated with Felix Draeseke. Back in 1851 Wagner's friend Theodor Uhlig called Schumann an 'absolute musician'. The view that Schumann was a master of Absolute Music, however grotesque it may appear to be, is still widely prevalent today.

The view that music and poesy—the 'romantic' arts—are closely related to one another is a fundamental idea of Romantic art theory. It is found very often in the Schlegel brothers, Jean Paul, E.T.A. Hoffmann and others, and follows logically from the principle that poesy is the quintessence of every art.

The idea of a union or even of a fusion of music and poesy is a key idea which several composers have tried to realize in different ways, leading to different solutions: with Schumann it led to the poeticizing of music (mainly instrumental music); with Wagner it led to the creation of the 'consummate artwork' or the great synthesis; and with Liszt, to the development of a definite species of programme music.

Robert Schumann's art theory was considerably influenced by the thinking of Jean Paul. Poesy is the uppermost authority in the aesthetic of both of them. The Poetic ('the idealistic world', according to Schumann) is the region of Art. Schumann defines music as 'the higher power of poesy'. In his letters and writings he never tired of postulating that a composer should be a poet and aspire for the poetic consciousness. In his writings he often used the terms 'poetic' and 'the Poetic'. Very often he differentiated the poetic side of music from the theoretical side and from the 'virtuosic' aspect.

'Poetic Music' (negatively at first) allows itself to be defined as the opposite of all music which is simply set on the escalation of outward and superficial virtuosity, wishing only to be a play on sound.

In Schumann's opinion Beethoven was the 'enemy of all that is mechanical'; to him Beethoven's work appeared to be the prototype of the 'purely poetic creation'. One of the goals that Schumann wished to pursue through the establishment of a new magazine for music was 'to help prepare and expedite the coming of a new poetic era'.

Poetic music is primarily Romantic music. According to Schumann, J.S. Bach was a precursor of Romanticism, and Beethoven and Schubert were genuine Romantics and pioneers of the Romantic School, which began to develop from 1830.

In the 'highest kind' of music, 'as it has been given to us in the individual creations' of Bach and Beethoven, Schumann thinks he can discover 'poetic depths and novelty everywhere—in the single parts as well as in the whole'. 'The poetry and humour combine in the depth of the newer music', he wrote to his friend Dr Gustav A. Keferstein on 31 January 1840, 'which has its origins more in Bach. In their music Mendelssohn, Bennett, Chopin, Hiller and all the so-called Romantics (the Germans, I always mean) stand much closer to Bach than to Mozart.'

'Poetic Music' is for Schumann, as for Hegel, 'the language of the soul'. Schumann sees the 'poetry' of music in the manifestation of the 'rare', 'noble' and 'secret' state of the soul. The predominance of the 'idea', the 'poetic material' and 'noble state of the soul' stands contrary to 'form domination', 'domination by trends', and philistinism.

Titles are especially justified with regard to the secret, inner state of the soul and also necessary. There are private conditions of the soul where a hint or a clue from the composer, in words, can lead to a quicker understanding and must be thankfully received.

Poetic music must always be full fantasy and also be capable of exciting the fantasy of the listener. Schumann took these fundamental ideas from the aesthetic theory of Jean Paul, who said, 'Fantasie is the highest of the poetic powers'.

As an art of 'poetic freedom', poetic music must be original, new and fantastic. Under poetic freedom Schumann understood a liberation from stiff, rigid schemata and a renewal of the Form and of the expression. In his opinion it was these qualities which distinguished the best works of the composers whom he considered to be Romantics in the main.

In Schumann's view, poetic music led one into the 'spiritual realm of Art', into the world of dreams. Music exercises 'its full powers' there, 'where it plays into the suprasensuous, transcendental world of the spiritual'. Hoffmann wrote in 1810, 'Music (instrumental) unlocks for man an unknown realm, a world which shares nothing with the outward material world of sense perception which surrounds him and in which he leaves behind all definable feelings, in order to abandon and yield himself to the inexpressible. And Beethoven's Fifth "which incorporates his Romanticism more than any other of his works", sweeps the listener "irresistibly" into the wonderful, spiritual realm of the infinite.'[1]

Poems may inspire one to compose, and conversely poetic music can inspire poetry. If we now take up the question of the ways in which Schumann's ideal of a poetic music manifests itself in his own compositions then we must keep in mind that several of his works carry titles and, as can be proved, these were suggested by personal experiences, picturesque ideas and literary impressions.

In a letter to Heinrich Dorn on 15 September 1839, Schumann admitted that personal experiences occasionally induced the coming into being of his works. 'Of course from all conflicts that Clara costs me some has been included in my music, and certainly it may be so understood by you. The Concert, the Sonata, the Davidsbündlertänze, the Kreisleriana have been initiated practically by her alone.'

Schumann received the inspiration to compose the First Symphony Op. 48 from a poem by Adolph Böttger. Originally titles had been thought of for each of the four movements, which were later withdrawn before publication.

In a letter to Simrock, Schumann recorded that his Third Symphony Op. 97, the one called *Rheinish* (1850), 'here and there probably reflects a piece of life'. The fourth movement originally carried the title 'in character of an accompaniment to a festive solemn ceremony'.

Schumann was the most consistent champion of the poetically inspired instrumental music in the nineteenth century. It would be incorrect to label him as an opponent of every sort of programme music. His reserved distance from the programme music of Berlioz can be traced back to three causes.

The first reason was Schumann's conviction that detailed, exhaustive programmes were evil, because they directed the fantasy of the listener into a fixed channel, leaving him no room for free unfolding. In this unavoidable 'suppression' of the listener's imagination Schumann saw nothing other than the violation of the rights of the delicate German listener, who, in contrast to the French, would not be so crudely led in his thinking. This is why he claimed that the main titles for the five movements of the Symphonie Fantastique would have been adequate. One may note that this statement nevertheless implies a concession, an acknowledgement. The second reason was Schumann's special aversion towards the programme of the Symphonie Fantastique. The third cause lay in Schumann's view that the artist has the right and the duty not to reveal the reason for and the process of his creation: 'Man possesses a native awe of the working place of a genius: he does not wish to know anything about the reasons, tools and secrets of the creative process. Nature also demonstrates a certain subtlety in that she covers her roots with earth; so should the artist conceal the throes of his labour. We would discover terrible things if we could see to the roots of the coming into being of a work.' If one reflects on this 'fundamental principle', one can well think that for Schumann the communication of the excessively 'personal' programme of the Symphonie Fantastique almost amounted to exhibitionism.

Schumann's observations about the purpose and the justification of 'titles' are therefore not self-contradictory—rather more, they allow one to recognize a sophisticated and discriminating way of thinking. Titles, which according to his concepts were justified by the subject, he held to be permissible or even necessary. From a few remarks of Schumann it emerges however that he sometimes had misgivings and a concern of a fundamental importance. He feared that titles or headings would limit the fantasy of the listener, and so allowed himself at times to be guided by the idea that the educated musicians did not require titles—for he thought him capable of understanding the character of the music and what is being intended by the composer without having to guess at it.

Recapitulating the data presented, the observations and the intermediate inferences, it becomes obvious that Schumann's musical 'poetic' can be condensed into four points:

1. Schumann subscribed to the conviction that music could and should express all things extra-musical. He allowed himself to be inspired to compose by literary impressions; he associated the literary and the visual with the musical and was fascinated by the idea of an 'opera without a text' and experienced in his own case how picturesque ideas arose during composition and influenced the creative process. However, Schumann was of the opinion that an instrumental composer ought not to begin his work with a fixed intent or resolution premeditated to convert a prefabricated 'programme' into music. Such a course of action violated his principle that the artistic process of creation is unconscious and inexplicable.
2. The main feature fundamental to Schumann's instrumental creation is the aspiration for the 'characteristic' and the 'poetic', under which Schumann understood the 'not mechanic', the 'romantic', the 'special', the 'unusual' and the 'secret', the fanciful and the fantastic, the New and the original—the 'dreamlike'. For the understanding of instrumental works, which had the 'special' as the subject, he held titles to be essential. As a result he disapproved, however, of the misuse that many of his contemporaries made of them and demanded that titles should measure to the content of the music and 'well out of the inner depths'.
3. Schumann allowed himself to be led by the concept that even the 'characteristic' and 'poetic' whose part he took, is at first to be assessed as music and evaluated according

to its rules. He repeatedly warned against the misunderstanding that a title (as an indication of the extra-musical 'content' of a composition) is a guarantee for, or an indication of the quality of the music. This is why he stated, 'The main issue remains—whether the music in itself is anything or excellent, whether its soul is in itself without the text and the elucidation.' To composers who wished to put the effectiveness and the quality of their extra-musically inspired works to test, Schumann suggested the removing of the titles just as an experiment.

4. As explained, Schumann held titles to be necessary, but he spoke out against the circulation of a detailed programme. He apparently arrived at this attitude through several considerations. He was afraid that a detailed programme allows no room for a play of fantasy to unfold freely. He believed that the artist has the duty and the right to conceal the reason for, and the procedure of his work from the public. And he subscribed to the view that elucidations of the content could be misunderstood in many ways.

From this exposition it should be clear that the difference between the poetically inspired creation of Schumann and programme music is in reality much smaller than is usually acknowledged. Many of Schumann's works are based on 'inner programmes' which Schumann, true to his principles, has encoded or withheld. The number of Schumann's compositions which could be classified as esoteric programme music is greater than one thinks.

In 1837 the 'Childrenscenes' Op. 15, came into being. The separation from Clara continued; Schumann was successful in capturing moments of association through a rare plasticity in the musical formulation. Not the process or the current of association is composed, but as in photography Schumann fixed the roving thoughts on to a moment. Diverse and always differently formulated, repetitions, sudden, pregnant brevity, and an almost unbelievable absence of formal intention allow the individual scenes to appear strangely self-evident and 'natural'. Where in the *Fantasie* Op. 17 the 'allowing oneself to be driven' was the centre, here the opposite holds true. Through recapitulation, one or two musical thoughts are so knit into one another that progress is not awaited; instead the underplayed, lightly hinted-at angle captivates the whole receptive faculty of the listeners. Many-sided intricacy gives way to vivid plasticity. Nothing is indicated by the pieces, but the music changes itself to 'children-scenes'. Schumann had added the thirteen titles later, but their thematic precision is already anticipated in the musical photography.

More problematic than the *Carnaval* or the *Kreisleriana,* is the *Humoreske* Op. 20 (1839). It was written towards the end of Schumann's stay in Vienna and expresses once for all the achievement and the exceptionality of Schumann's piano music. In autumn 1838 Schumann went to Vienna, encouraged by Clara to start a new music magazine there. But the Vienna interlude did not work out as planned. Schumann found the Metternich repression crippling and paralysing. The censorship reminded him 'exactly of the time of the vehme (Fehme)': 'one may not speak what one thinks.'

Till 1840 the whole phase of piano music is marked by the literary and the poetic. Schumann, who had vacillated at the start between the career of a writer and the career of a musician, wrote poems in music to a certain extent. This music has the general appearance of the narrative, the 'poetic speaking'. The unbelievable multifacetedness of the poetic cycles has its origins in this tendency of narrative fantasizing. It is not an illustration of nor composed after a literary text but a whole world of poetic fancies which has transformed itself and has become music.

The *Humoreske* expresses a fullness of rhetorical attitudes but always as music. It is never possible to solve its mystery in a literary programme. For Schumann, the quality of the poetic is exactly contained in the secret, enigmatic language of music. 'Music is the higher power of Poetry; the Angels must speak in musical tones and Spirits in the words of Poesy.' Schumann speaks of music as being the spiritual language of feeling.

If the *Carnaval* excels shiningly in the art of characterizing, which finally made it the most famous piece of Schumann's piano music, something else holds true for the *Humoreske*: rhetoric, emotions, passions. None of the many parts allows itself to be equally and precisely understood, as does for example 'Chopin' or 'Paganini' from the *Carnaval*. One can also not speak of a movement sequence, while the sense of the whole context comes into being through extension, through the different illumination or rhythmization. Schumann tends to narrate more in order to allow himself to be brought always to newer innuendoes and associations. When the Polonaise-rhythm is touched 'with some pomp' then a Polonaise dance is not created, but a grandiose, rhetorically effective rhythmic emotion appears, without carrying a development in itself.

The speed with which the musical 'poesy' changes its themes and 'pictures', colours and tones, compels the listener to experience each figure as the present, without having the assurance of meeting a form or thought again.

Schumann defines the concept of the *Humoreske* in narrow and static terms. 'The French do not understand the word "Humoreske". It is terrible that exactly for the most deeply rooted concepts and peculiarities—as for "Gemütliche (Schwärmerische)" and for "humor"—which is the happy fusion of Gemütliche and Witzig—there is no fitting word available in the French language.' The piece however steadfastly demands new views and sights, and new sounds. Each attitude reveals itself as the wrapping, the envelope of another; each movement can be broken up or put into a parenthesis; the appeal or call can end in melancholic meditation; the gay and tipsy small talk can change itself to vigorous gesticulation.

This coming into being and breaking off, this spinning on further, demands a high-level presence and flexibility also from the interpreters.

The elementary principle of this further fantasizing poses problems for the finale. The last piece is explicitly entitled 'Zum Beschlusse' (conclusion), without being able to find and end straightaway. Schumann interrupts this strange inner moving force of reflection and brooding with an abrupt and peremptory gesture. This process of fantasizing emotions, of the rhetoric-poetic fantasy, is demonstrated in Schumann's observation to Clara about the creation of the *Humoreske*. 'The whole week I sat at the piano and composed and wrote and laughed and cried confusedly; you will find all this portrayed in my Op. 20—the "great Humoreske" . . .'

1 E.T.A. Hoffmann, *Schriften zur Musik,* hrsg. von Friedrich Schnapp, Winkler Verlag, München 1963.

Симфония № 7

Liszt

1

If one looks into the research done on Liszt, one cannot escape coming to the conclusion that Liszt has been a 'victim of his biographers'. In all of Western Music history, Franz Schubert is probably the only other composer to have been treated with a similarly persistent lack of understanding. For example in 1975 in the periodical *Neue Musik* Hans Vogt claimed that 'there had been salon-gypsies of the variety of Liszt and that today there are musical salon-Indians.' Liszt was contemptuously classified as belonging to the field of 'Entertainment Music'. With his Liszt biography in 1931, Peter Raabe accomplished a great biographical achievement; and his two-volume work formed a very important contribution towards the reparation of a piece of music history gone astray.

One might be aware of the fact that the later works of Liszt were for long almost completely unknown (the late piano works only became available through three publications of the English Liszt Society in 1950 and 1957). Even Raabe, prejudiced by the negative evaluation of Hans von Bülow, found in Liszt's later works symptoms of creative decline.

On the whole Liszt was portrayed as a *richly-faceted artistic personality,* who took for his own the expansive awareness of life of French Romanticism.

To begin with, there were the two famous female companions of Liszt—the Countess d'Agoult and Cardyne von Sayn-Wittgenstein, who, each in her own way, as mentioned in the first Liszt biography by Julius Kapp (1909), treated Liszt as a Super-being. Liszt was elevated to the 'best of all men, the greatest of all artists, the profoundest of all philosophers, the most pious of all Christians'. These personality clichés stem from the fact that Liszt himself did a lot towards concealing his true person. His narcissistic self-presentation and heterogeneous identity incorporated the expansive features of French Romanticism, and came to include the Bohemian, the Dandy, the Snob, the Libertine, the Penitent and the Abbé. In his cosmopolitanism Liszt showed great enthusiasm for the most varied cultural influences. He was interested in mysticism, in the Cabbalah, Freemasonry, Pantheism, and even in the newest findings in the Natural Sciences. All this led to the great notice taken of this personality by writers of trivial literature and kitsch-biographers and even by great authors such as Balzac, Heine, George Sand. Almost every author and writer of memoirs in the last century described or at least mentioned Liszt. He was known all over Europe, and above all in the art criticism of the German-language regions (chiefly represented by Robert Schumann) which did not find itself in sympathy with the emotion-drenched ambience of French Romanticism. The criticism was also carried out on a personal level. His love-affairs especially were traced in detail by the writers of salon-literature (even as late as 1971: E. K. Horvath, *Women around Liszt*). In her scientifically authenticated biography, Klara Hamburger attempts to establish that Liszt, in the years that he lived with C. von Sayn-Wittgenstein, was totally under her influence, the testimonies of this fact provided by the choice of themes, by the heroic-pathetic themes of the Weimar period. The aphoristic comment by Nietzsche is well known: 'Liszt—the School of Velocity—chasing women'.

What is interesting is that the aforementioned cosmopolitanism of Liszt grew into a problem. In his book, *The Man Liszt* (1934), Ernest Newman wrote that it was precisely this cosmopolitanism that constituted the tragic component of his life and left him homeless with his European music-language. At a time which saw the growth of nationalistic consciousness, the internationalism of Liszt's musical thinking presented a constant stumbling-block. The petty parochialism of patriotism lay behind the rejection of Liszt's work, especially during the Weimar period. Liszt lived at a time of violent social upheavals.

We are thus faced by the contradictions between two stages of development in the organization of society, viz. between the

Bruckner meets Wagner : a contemporary caricature.

Bruckner as the 'German Michel' : a contemporary caricature.

Schonberg : as painted by Egon Schiele, 1917.

Webern : as painted by Oskar Kokoschka, 1914.

feudal way of life and the bourgeois emancipation from the traditional theocratic heritage. So, on the one side we see a personality, who, for the sake of self-preservation, adheres to the socially higher classes and who assimilates the feudal way of life into himself. In contrast to this stands the identification with the Saint Simon social movement and with the Christian Socialism of Lamennais. And it is equally difficult to reconcile his enthusiastic identification with the goals of French Romanticism, which tried to break the feudal chains of the *ancien régime,* with his sense of belonging to the aristocracy.

However, as we turn to the musician Liszt, among his works we find a Revolution-symphony (1830) and a piano-work with the title 'Lyon' (1835). Already in his early works Liszt attempts to anticipate the ideas of the Weimar period, to renew the music through an inner bond with poesy. Already here it is possible to see the beginnings of Liszt's typical monothematic method of composition, to develop and construct a whole composition out of a single 'germ-cell'. As is known, Liszt adhered to one of the most important principles of style in Romanticism: the musicalization of the word. Music becomes verbal and acquires a speech-like Gestalt (form).

In his theoretical writings Liszt aired his views on the function of Art and Music. Music has the task of stepping out from the public-forum/aristocratic forms of performance in order to be able to devote itself to the needs of the people. Art is understood as the expressive humanization of true religion. Liszt devoted himself his whole life long to the the mediation of Art and Religion.

2

THE FAUST SYMPHONY

The *Faust Symphony* composed in 1854 counted and still counts as one of Franz Liszt's most significant works. Also acknowledged as one of Liszt's chief compositions by his opponents, the *Faust Symphony* belongs to a time of violent conflict between the Modern Germans and the Conservatives, and was predestined to become an object of controversy.

The New Germans place this work above everything that had been created in the field of symphonic music after Beethoven until then. In 1862 the music author Richard Pohl said that there was nothing worthier of being placed alongside Beethoven's last and great work than this *Faust Symphony*.

Among Conservatives, E. Hanslick was of the opinion that the first movement of this composition was nothing more than a 'disappointing piece of patchwork', and was almost 'peculiar'—'a botched-up Berlioz who thought he was Goethe'.

The reactions of A. Bruckner, R. Strauss, and Bela Bartok however, were almost euphoric.

Substantial research and investigation have been carried out on this symphony, with two questions coming up again and again:

(1) Are no allusions to the scenes and events of the dramatic action, to be found in the symphony?

(2) Is it possible to make precise, verifiable comments about the semantics of the music and about Liszt's view and understanding of the Faust material?

In 1981, Peter Raabe evolved an original thesis, according to which, Liszt's work reflected personal experiences and views. The first movement is seen to be a self-avowal, the Gretchen-movement is supposed to enlighten one about Liszt's view of the 'Eternal Woman'. Raabe bases his theory on letters. But, as it happens so often in the field of research, the wish or the desire is often father to the thought. Newer analyses have since shown that these interpretations are false. In actuality, Liszt felt a greater sympathy towards Byron's Manfred and not wholly without ethical reasons, for he held against Faust his cowardly desertion of Gretchen.

On the other hand, it is generally known that Liszt did sometimes change his opinion on literary questions. While he was certainly not an indiscriminate admirer of Goethe, on the title-page of the Symphony Liszt described it clearly as 'a Faust-Symphony after Goethe'.

The Faust Movement

A fundamental principle of Liszt's symphonic programme-music was the dictum that the subject of a composition (the poetic idea) must determine the form. By following this basic principle, Liszt sought to liberate his music from the schematic of the 'classical form' and to throw open for his music unlimited possibilities for the formal gestalting. However, viewed from a distance, this content-form relation does not become immediately apparent.

The sequence of the movements allows one to catch glimpses of the Ninth Symphony, which acted as a model.

Three instrumental movements—

First movement (Faust)
slow movement (Gretchen)
Scherzo (Mephisto)
—are followed by a Finale with a male-choir and tenor-solo.

Each of the three movements is based upon unique individual themes, the number of which varies from movement to movement (The Faust movement is based on five themes, the Gretchen movement on two, and the Mephisto movement is based upon some gestalts which characterize Mephisto). In the Gretchen and Mephisto movements, the Faust theme reappears. Now, this method of gestalting does not obey pure-musical principles, but is subject to a 'poetic necessity'.

If, in the middle section of the Gretchen movement, Liszt once more takes up the Faust theme, he intends with this to show that Faust has entered into Gretchen's world. When in the Mephisto movement he reverses the Faust theme into a negative form, he intends to underline clearly the fact that he has adopted Goethe's characterization of Mephisto for his own: Mephisto, the 'spirit of contradiction', cannot create anything on his own, but can only 'negate' and 'destroy'.

The five strongly contrasting themes of the Faust movement are structured differently and profiled sharply with great skill.

Theme I: augmented triad, sighing motifs
3 groups of motifs
Motif group 1a = 'dodecaphonic theme'
1b = sighing phrase of the oboes, clarinets and bassoons
1c = sighing motif on the violins

This theme became famous, because it did not allow itself to be classified by the rules of Functional Harmonic theory. The notes 'a' flat and 'e' form the tonal centres.

After a considerably 'long pause' the theme is brought forward a second time. The theme bears the features of a monologue.

Theme II : Contrast to Theme I
key—c-minor, wholly harmonized and of passionate character.
The three-note sighing motif of Theme I is also one of the elements here.

Theme III : Dramatic-recitative character:
a four, correspondingly five-bar sighing-melodic phrase played in different variations, alternately in the high and low ranges by oboes, clarinets on the one side, and by bassoons, violoncelli and double-basses on the other. The second violins and violas accompany in tremolo.

Theme IV : dolente-group from Theme I
change from 3/4 time to 4/4 time
E-major, change to c-minor

Theme V : Laid out in a dualistic way:
antecedent phrase contrasting strongly with the consequent phrase (4/4–3/4)

The augmented triad as the emblem of Faust

Ernest Newman in 1946 aired the possibility that Liszt is likely to have received the inspiration for the augmented triad of the Faust movement from the theories of his Berlin friend Carl Friedrich Weizmann, who in 1853 (a year before the symphony was written), brought out a book about the augmented triad. In the case of Liszt however, the augmented triad at the beginning of the Faust symphony appears wholly without a functional connection—this is the first case in the history of music where this happens. These triads are however not atonal.

To all appearances the first movement of the Faust symphony is the first in the history of music to be constructed upon the relations/proportions which result from the division of the Octave into three equal parts.

What semantic function do the augmented triad and the major-third relationship have in the *Faust Symphony*?

Semantics

Richard Pohl's procedure was as follows: to comment upon the themes and the individual parts of the symphony with verses from Goethe's tragedy. Pohl started from the assumption that the five themes of the Faust movement fittingly reflect and characterize the main features of the Faust character, and he went on to characterize the themes as follows:

Theme I : characterizes the basic features of the Faust-figure, of his Being—namely, doubt, grief, discontent, moodiness, contempt for the world and for science, as well as his own aspiration and the hopeless emptiness of his inner soul.

Theme II : is seen as the theme of 'the passionate urge', desire for higher knowledge, for great deeds, the restlessness and the struggling for freedom/liberation.

Theme III : the theme of 'burning longing for unknown happiness', a plea to be redeemed from inner pain and torture.

Theme IV : the theme of Love; as universal Godly and human love.

Theme V : the theme of 'Pride, the mighty consciousness of the highest perception'.

Pohl's procedure was subjective—despite this the later hermeneutic commentators based themselves upon him.

If one examines the question of the way in which the music makes it possible to acquire knowledge about its semantics, one can come to the conclusion that the immense expressiveness of the music determined by contrasts, lends expression to the complexity and the contradictiveness of the Faustian nature.

The five themes characterize different aspects of Faust's personality.

The dodecaphonic theme is linked to Faust's learning, to his urge for higher knowledge, to the brooding nature of his character.

Theme II characterizes his passionate and unbridled nature, his violent being, his attraction towards contrasts.

Themes III and IV show him as a creature in suffering and pain.

Finally, theme V characterizes the Splendid and the Eternal in this man.

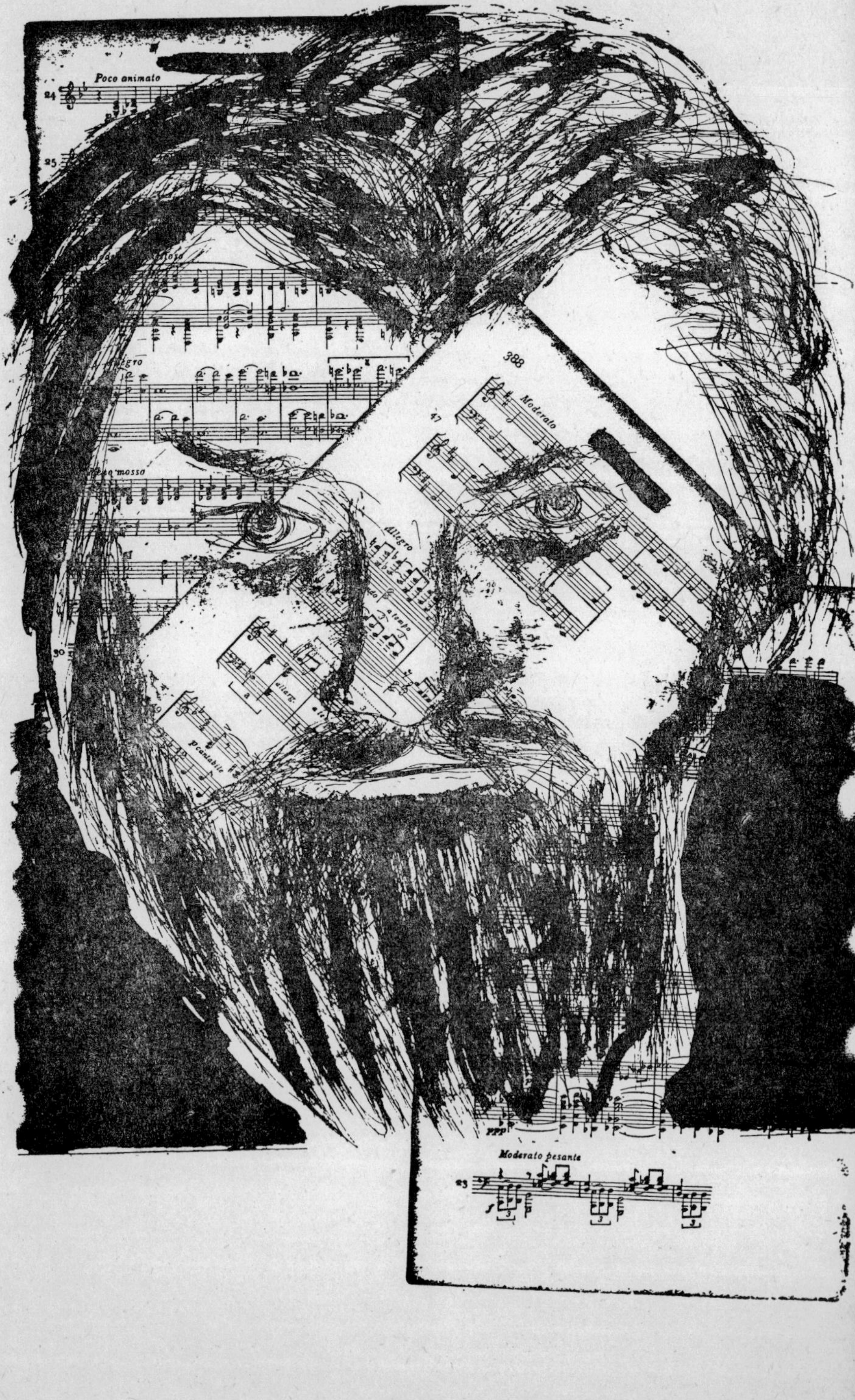
Poco animato
388
Moderato
Allegro
a tempo
p cantabile
Moderato pesante

Brahms and the Heritage of Beethoven

On 1 October 1853 Clara Schumann, the wife of Robert Schumann, wrote in her diary: 'This month brought us a wonderful appearance in Brahms, the twenty year old composer from Hamburg. He is once again one of those who seem to be specially sent by God. He played us his own sonatas, scherzos etc. all full of exuberant fantasy, intimacy of emotion and mastery in form. Robert says, he knows of nothing that he can say to him, of nothing that he should leave out of his work or add to it. It is really moving, when one sees this young man at the piano, his interesting youthful face, which is absolutely transfigured while playing, his beautiful hands which overcome the greatest difficulties with ease. (His pieces are very difficult.) And then to add to all this these curious compositions. A bright future stands before him because it is only when he finally writes for the orchestra will he have found the right field for his fantasy. Robert says, "One can wish for no more than to hope that heaven keeps him healthy!" '

Along with Hugo Wolf and Gustav Mahler, Johannes Brahms numbers among the most literary and educated composers of the late Romantic period. Throughout his long life he was possessed by a passion for reading, the dimensions of which can be gathered from his collection of quotations, 'The young Kreisler's Treasure Chest'. He had a special affinity with the German Romantics, especially Jean Paul, E.T.A. Hoffmann, Novalis and Eichendorff, and in his youth he identified himself with Hoffmann's orchestra conductor Kreisler. Brahms had a good command of political literature unlike Bruckner whom he considered to be 'crazy and uneducated'. Brahms is usually taken to be a prototype of the enlightened Protestant. He was considered to be 'deeply religious' and as a Lutheran belonged to the evangelical culture circle, well versed in the Bible; and from his aversion to dogmatically confined religion, he was above religion, tolerant to the point of being liberal and a free-thinker.

Any characterization of Brahms and his music almost invariably leads to a comparison with Bruckner. There are significant differences particularly in their works for the choir which also allow for some general conclusions. A major difference lies in their individual relationship to what can be termed the Gregorianic. With Bruckner and Liszt the Gregorianic is doubtlessly an important factor. In contrast, in the spiritual choral creations of Brahms it was hardly allowed to be of significance. Bruckner as well as Brahms had a close relationship to the polyphony of the sixteenth and seventeenth centuries. In this, however, it is noteworthy that Bruckner tended more towards Palestrina while Brahms preferred to orient himself towards Heinrich Schütz. With regard to Bach, his influence on Brahms can hardly be overstressed, while his effect on Bruckner can hardly be proved precisely. The facts therefore point towards this, that in his spiritual vocal creations the Protestant Brahms attached himself mainly to the oeuvre of the Protestant musicians Schütz and Bach.

The relationship between Brahms and Bruckner was full of biting observations about each other. Brahms had recognized Bruckner's talent but he considered it to be Bruckner's ill fortune that he had fallen victim to Wagnerism. 'Do look,' said Brahms, indicating the first page of a Bruckner score, 'there the man invents as if he were Schubert, and then it strikes him that he is a Wagnerian, and everything goes to the Devil.' Bruckner behaved more defensively and once remarked, 'He is Brahms—and all respect! I am Bruckner—but my pieces are preferable to me! And whoever wishes to be moved by music cannot be satisfied by Brahms' music.'

Brahms and Bruckner

When we now take a look at the historical situation it is brought home to us that the Brahms-Bruckner antithesis had only in fact unleashed the much older conflict between Brahms and Wagner. Brahms correctly observed that after his death in 1883 the Wagner party required a new leader and as such for the want of someone better, Bruckner was raised on to the banner. In essence the ideological war had four aspects:

1. *The quarrel between the music of the future and absolute music*
One of the axioms that belonged among the most important rules of the art history system of Richard Wagner was that after Beethoven's Ninth Symphony a further development of absolute music and the symphony was no longer possible, and that the Ninth could only be directly followed by the 'consummate artwork' of the future—the integrated drama, to which Beethoven had already forged the key. On this basis for the followers of Wagner, the music of the future could only unfold in two fields, viz. 'that of the music drama and that of the symphonic poem'. Chamber music was not looked upon highly by these followers, despite Wagner's regard for Beethoven's later quartets. They considered it to be a 'lesser genre' while the opposition was confident that especially with Brahms it was in the best possible care.

2. *The antithesis between heteronomic and autonomic aesthetics*
The terminology mentioned here refers in essence to the old pair of concepts, content and form. The question is: is music determined out of itself by purely formal rules or is this determination or development of the music governed by a definite relation to a poetic thought?

3. *The conflict between inspiration and the skill of artistic realization*
In the Romantic period inspiration was an important category of the expression of the creative genius. Schumann, Wagner, Liszt, Bruckner swore by the paramount relevance of their Inspiration. Set against this, Brahms' conviction that the artistic performance did not lie in 'Inspiration' which he awaited as a 'gift', but in the realization of it, made an anachronistic impression. Brahms is reported to have said in conversation: 'That what one actually calls invention, i.e. a real thought, is so to say a higher inspiration, i.e. I can do

nothing for it. I must make that gift through incessant work into my own rightful property. With the thought it is as with a seed: it sprouts unconsciously in one's innermost self.'

Brahms was repeatedly criticized by his opponents who said that his technical mastery concealed a weakness in inventiveness and originality. He was characterized as a master of emulation, as a person with ability who had nothing original to say. The author of these opinions, which created prejudice amongst many of Brahms' contemporaries, was none other than the great Wagner. A parallel to this situation is to be found in the pair Schönberg-Stravinsky. In Schönberg's opinion Stravinsky was an unoriginal 'disguise artist' who had cut his hair as a 'page boy' in order to look exactly like 'Papa Bach'.

4. *The conflict between progressiveness and traditionalism*

Wagner once apostrophized: 'Children! Do new things! new! and always new! If you hang on to the old you will be possessed by the devil of unproductivity, and you will be the saddest of artists!' Wagner considered progress to be the 'course of development of all mankind'. 'The return to antiquity' appeared to him to be artificial. This, however, has nothing to do with contempt for tradition. Wagner's reverence for tradition was genuine. But neither Wagner nor Liszt was what one calls anti-historical. Wagner always described the best works of Gluck, Mozart and Beethoven as forerunners of the art of the future.

Brahms' reverence for tradition was so powerful that one might almost speak of an inferiority complex. He was absolutely convinced that music had already achieved its zenith before him. He declined to speak about the 'Revolutionaries' who had gathered around Richard Strauss and prophesied the decline of art. Against this background Brahms' almost extreme preference for the Variations and the Passacaglia-form, his fondness for the Fugue, the strict movement technique and the contrapuntal technique of the older music becomes understandable.

As mentioned, Brahms was considered by the Wagnerians to be a disguise artist. Hugo Wolf called him 'an eclectic' Nietzche, 'a style copier', an epigon, an inferior imitator. 'The musical politicians of our time,' writes Philipp Spitta, 'call him a reactionary'. Brahms' enthusiastic followers indeed held him to be the legitimate heir of Beethoven and fought for this conviction. 'If his music at all reminds one of anything, it is of the later Beethoven.' The catch-phrase that Brahms was Beethoven's real successor, was set in circulation, as it appears, by Hans von Bülow. He was the one who, after his estrangement from Wagner, gave Brahms' First Symphony at the performance in Hanover the title 'The Tenth' and he also coined the popular phrase, 'The three great B's,' for Bach, Beethoven, Brahms. Against this it is interesting to compare Nietzsche's comment: 'One gladly calls Brahms the heir of Beethoven, I know of no more cautious euphemism.'

Beethoven's Tenth

Johannes Brahms, the connoisseur and admirer of Beethoven, had his consciousness so permeated by the outstanding performance of his ideal that his creative potential suffered under this. Nothing is more characteristic of his inferiority complex with regard to Beethoven as the famous remark to Hermann Levi: 'I will never compose a symphony! You have no idea of how it is for one of us, when he always hears such a giant (Beethoven) marching behind him.'

Under these circumstances one is not surprised to discover that it was performances of Beethoven's Ninth Symphony which generated the urge to create symphonies in Brahms as well as Bruckner. Brahms heard it for the first time in March 1854 in Cologne, under Ferdinand Hiller. The impression was so powerful that shortly after Brahms began to compose the symphonically inspired D-minor sonata. Later out of this as an interim phase emerged the symphonic version of the first movement, which finally developed as the piano concerto Op. 15.

The first symphony of Brahms is committed not only to the Ninth, but to several of Beethoven's symphonies. The Fifth it has a lot to thank for, for it is in the same key. Next to this it shows connections to the *Eroica,* to the Seventh and to the Second *Leonore* Overture. We hear an expressive Oboes and

Flute theme at the end of the *Un poco sostenuto*, which recalls the Marcia Funebre of the *Eroica.*

Brahms and Form

Brahms was praised as well as criticized for his ability to produce an astonishing amount out of the germ cell of a single thematic thought through 'developing variations'. None less than Arnold Schönberg confessed to having learnt 'economy and richness in spite of it' among other things, from Brahms. A remarkably illustrative example of the Brahmsian capability of developing a multifaceted whole out of a little is offered by the first movement of the first symphony. The connections in between the main theme, which is a 'double theme', the side theme and the 'end group', is so close that one may well speak of an inclination towards monothematism.

Johannes Brahms is perhaps the most significant representative of the stricter direction that the variation composition took in the nineteenth century after the Beethoven era. His variation creations develop further in the direction initiated by Beethoven. The music-author Luithlen said that 'Brahms had strengthened what he had found in Beethoven, enlarged it and individually interpreted it with depth. He had filled the variations form with highly personal content.' To be sure Brahms never neglected the connection between poetry and music, on occasions he even called himself a poet and differentiated clearly between the genres of his Tonepoesie. 'In general the symphony represented for him the dramatic; the chamber music the epic; the song the lyric form.' Many of Brahms' remarks indicate that he had adopted a lot of Schumann's Aesthetic of Poetry for himself.

Brahms the man

Brahms' identification with E.T.A. Hoffmann's character of the young orchestra conductor has already been mentioned (Hoffmann's novel is carried by the idea and the belief in the regenerative power of art), which was for him the essential meaning of fanatical artistry, a synonym for 'the love of Art, and 'enthusiasm', which did not submit to opposition and disappointment.

Stillness, silence, shyness characterize one side of Brahms' nature; excitability, lack of phlegm, passion, a tendency towards extravagance, a weakness for the bizarre inspiration, humour, irony, and even sarcasm, his other side—and further the joy in a convivial togetherness with a few friends, and the last but not the least, the relentless self-criticism, which saved his own creations from destruction when he was convinced that he had achieved the highest possible degree of perfection.

The following passage from the foreword to *Kreisleriana* is almost like a characterization of the 'mature' Brahms. 'It also happened that friends could not understand how he (Johannes Kreisler) wrote down a composition, or having written it down, left it undestroyed. Sometimes he wrote in the night in the most excited mood; he woke the friend who lived near him, in order to play it to him, all in the highest spirits—he wept tears of joy over the successful work—he praised himself as the happiest man, but on the next day—the splendid composition lay in the fire.'

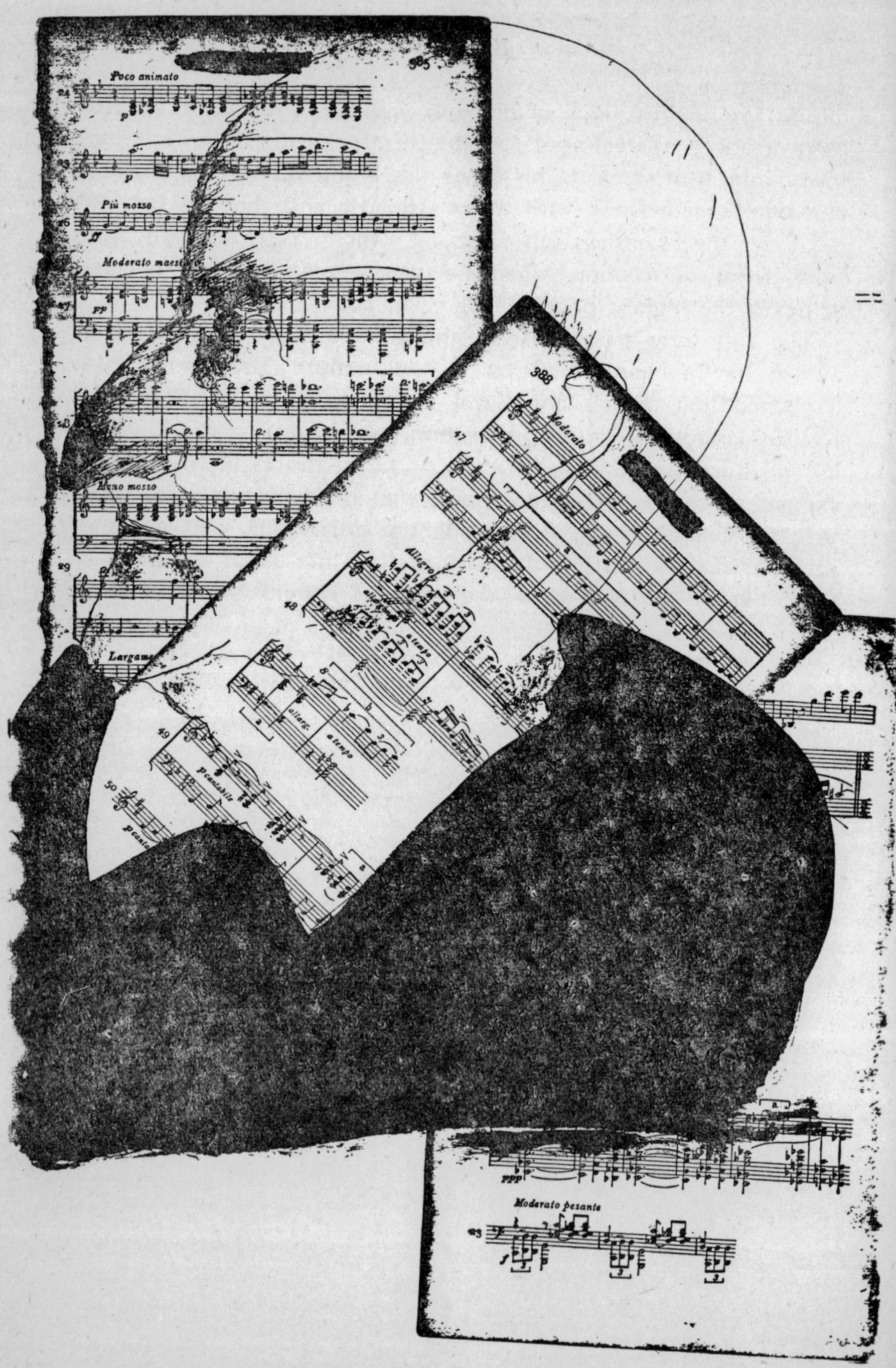

385
Poco animato
Più mosso
Meno mosso
388
Moderato
Allegro
a tempo
p cantabile
Moderato pesante

Anton Bruckner: Attempt at a Psychogram

Several mistakes have been made in the evaluation of Anton Bruckner as a result of factional fights in the world of music in the nineteenth century. The relationship between Wagner and Bruckner is in fact much more complicated and multifaceted than one had thought it to be for a long time. The title of 'The Mystic of Music' appears to be prejudicial. In contrast to Wagner, Bruckner offers no endless melody construction; instead there is an additive 'Gestalting' (forming) in the micro-and the macrocosms, a sharp structuring of the groups of motifs and the tonal groups and a strict construction of the different groups of bars.

Further Bruckner has been considered an 'impulsive queer bird', hence his comments on the Fourth and Eighth symphonies were not taken seriously for a long time, although, as later demonstrated through research, they are indispensable for a deeper understanding of his music. The influence of Liszt and Berlioz on the gestalting (arranging) of the movements too was underestimated for a long time. The Brucknerians classified the music as 'unconditional', which led to his music being regarded as 'autonomous', i.e. devoid of any social determinants, in other words, asocial. But the Bruckner symphonies were composed in extremely contradictory and inconsistent social situations. Several biographers take no account of Bruckner's difficult identity problem. They state as their reason for not doing so that 'the life does not say anything about the work and the work nothing about the life'. This approach is antidialectic and easy to invalidate and refute. One does better to interpret Bruckner's oeuvre as an expression of his life and times.

The approach in this case lies in the idea that Bruckner's personality structure is a crystallization of a specific process of socialization in which the feudal interaction between master and slave was of great significance. In Austria in the Vormärz (the period before the revolution of March 1848) an authoritarian upbringing tended to form personality structures which would support the Metternich dictatorship. This was the typical Restoration upbringing that drilled in a norm of social behaviour *vis-á-vis* the religious and secular authorities anchoring and establishing in the character of the people the dictatorial conditions. Only one single time did Anton Bruckner protest against the inhuman working conditions in his capacity as an assistant in a school in Windhaag. Even after he had moved to Vienna he hung on to his submissive behaviour. As a lecturer at the Vienna University however he grew into the role of the aggressor and came to demonstrate contempt and intolerance.

Bruckner's lack of interest in practical politics has been emphasized in several biographies. He appeared to remain unaffected by the political upheavals of the time. The roots of this denial of interest in politics probably lie in the upbringing which neglected political and historical education during the Vormärz period. It can also however be related to an instinctive anxiety to hold everything that could threaten his existence at bay, without indeed being able to elude the danger.

Bruckner came from a petit-bourgeois milieu, a family of teachers. All the members of the family had to pool their income together to maintain a minimum level of existence. In the milieu of the St Florian Institution which suppressed all drives and impulses, sexuality was burdened with the curse of sin. With smug complacence, authors report on Bruckner's sexual behaviour which certainly reflects the result of the influences of the prevalent social character of the bourgeoisie of the nineteenth century. The identity of the living and working processes which was valid for the feudal system of production breaks up in the currents of industrial production and accelerated urbanization. The value system of the upper class and educated bourgeoisie with its emphasis on a regulated form of family life was adopted in many parts of the society.

The division into the private and the public calls for a new definition of roles. For centuries handled like little adults, children are *brought up*, to become in the process susceptible and exposed to the sufferings of the psyche. Human beings, in whom the disposition for neurotic illnesses go hand in hand with creativity and heightened performance ability, also grow up in such kinds of relationships.

The motherly demand for perfectionism casts a titanic pressure which stirs up disquiet and stimulates attempts to strive for the unattainable. Bruckner's narcissism combined with great illusory fantasies of being forced to break out of the petit-bourgeois milieu. At the same time he suffered from deep disturbances in his awareness of the self which tore his ego with melancholy crises of dejection and exuberant fantasies of greatness, evident in his dedications of works from the 'Master of Masters' (Wagner) to 'Beloved God'.

Bruckner was convinced of his place in the history of the development of music. But a categorization of his personal style does not suffice to characterize the man Bruckner. Without taking into account political upheavals and the accelerated progress of industrialization around him the development of his identity as a composer cannot be explained.

As the cathedral-organist in the state-capital of Linz he could widen considerably the horizons of his life. He came in contact with many dogmatic dignitaries who influenced him. In 1855 he joined a singing club in Linz, one with all the features of bourgeois uprightness. The petit-bourgeoisie lulls itself with gaiety and merriment. The works Bruckner composed at this time are either upright bourgeois or patriotic. Between them and the monumental symphonies lies a gigantic chasm.

The 'Wagner Experience' can be identified as the fountainhead of several of these symphonic outpourings. The disconcerting insecurity he felt before the avant-garde of that period—Liszt and Wagner, functional harmony, and chromaticism—led to a severe crisis of authority and tradition. The unnerving feeling of living in a state in which all the hitherto valid laws of music appeared no longer to hold true almost drew him on to the brink of madness. In 1867 he suffered from a powerful depression for which he was treated through a three month long cure. Between 1862 and 1867 his compository practice was marked by a new character. He allowed himself to be lured by Wagner's sensuality of sound. The effects of his psychological and spiritual illness were of a manifold nature leading him to equate Wagner with God. From this time on he composed his *Grosse Form* works for the bourgeois concert hall, for the bourgeois public—for their recognition was important to him. And yet he was not like Brahms a composer for the liberal bourgeoisie. Historically in 1867 the German-Austrian bourgeoisie was granted a privileged social position by the December Laws. In the Gründerzeit (foundation period of rapid expansion) following upon it, whole areas of the living surroundings were fundamentally changed through expansion in transport facilities, iron and heavy industries. Bruckner's monumental style carries unmistakable signs of the time. The 'Wagner-experience' alone is not an adequate explanation for the form he devised. In his choice of the secular form of the symphony Bruckner's allegiance to the monarchy did play a role. This is to be seen in the dedications of his works. Wholly in the spirit of a constitutional monarchy his works formulate a social compromise in that they bring monarchy and liberalism into unison.

Nietzsche's phrase, 'the revaluing of all values', as the aim defined for the Gründerzeit or foundation period did not leave Art and Music untouched, even when a creative artist expressly and verbally stated that the social upheavals did not interest him in the least. In the medium of the formative arts of literature and music, the progressive Americanization and concretization of the living world finds expression in the accentuation of the form-related constructional thought. With Johannes Brahms, Anselm Feuerbach, Hans von Marees, Conrad F. Mayer and finally Bruckner, the Gründerzeit high spirits of the seventies had a powerful impact which with the beginning of the Great Depression in 1873 soured into disenchantment and abysmal desperation.

There was an affinity between Bruckner's personal reorientation and the improving and perfecting of his monumental style. Brahms and Bruckner placed constructivism against the eruption of sudden, inspiring ideas. Beethoven hovers as a shadow over them both. In no part of Bruckner's scores is there any suggestion of Wagner's technique of endless melody. Like the protagonists of the formative arts and literature Bruckner prefers antithetical moods and contrast formation, through which he breaks into linear dynamism.

The range of his music conceived under the spirit of the Baroque that conceives a unity of earthly and heavenly cosmos is not conceived only to praise God. It also contains areas which express the fears and the concerns of the time, e.g. the Scherzo of Symphony 8. The unpolished rough brittleness of Bruckner's music demands a study of its language in terms other than those formulated by the various spiritual-historical interpretations, e.g. the desperately unhappy mood (the first movement of the Eighth Symphony), the 'Farewell from Life' (the Ninth Symphony), and so on.

At the end of 1867, close to lunacy, Bruckner began to count everything; his drives could only be curbed by a compulsive and obsessive quantification. Everything which could draw him from the correct path was to be warded off by the magic of counting. The quantifying passion affected his music, leading to the counting off of the periods, and the schematic division of the different groups of bars. The main theme from the first movement of the Seventh Symphony is the extreme limit of Bruckner's melody construction. It hardly takes account of the 'quadratic development of phrases'. In the beginning of the Symphony No. 9, to use an expression from Schönberg, he discards the corset of formal melodies to let the music breathe free. His ego was deeply hurt by the rejection of a symphony. As a rule he started to rework the score, examined all the periods, in that he counted the bars and numbered them through. He then checked the compositions for forbidden unisons or octave-parallels. He did not seek to find explanations for the rejections of his works in the work itself, but in himself in that he had not corresponded to the requirements of the principles of authority. The result of his formalism is that many feel that his music lacks warmth, life, spontaneity and humour. There is a stiffness and constraint in the inflection; the feelings and emotions of his music work intellectually without touching the heart.

Bruckner's necrophilia is reflected in the de-fleshing of his themes. Everything which still carries the promise of life starts to die away: a skeleton is left behind as evidence of the lifelong mortification of desire and longing. His was a life dedicated to Death. In the finale of Symphony No. 3 a polka and a choral are heard simultaneously. There, where Bruckner speaks out his fundamental melancholy authentically without distancing himself from its power through his ratio or intellect, there he can enthrall and captivate us wholly and completely.

Bruckner and German Michel

'The sense of every message is, however, further conditioned by the actual conditions under which it is communicated, and a knowledge of these actual conditions is presupposed in the persons at whom this message is directed. In order to understand a message one must imagine himself in these real conditions. A written work, for example, obtains its real significance only in context, with possible imaginations of the time in which it was created.'—August Boekh.

The most important source for information about the programme of the Eighth symphony is a letter from Bruckner to the famous conductor, Felix Weingartner, written on 21 January 1891:

> Once more I ask, how does the Eighth sound?
>
> In the first movement the trumpet and horn arrangement consists of the rhythm of the theme: the prophecy of Death, which appears always in a sporadic fashion; finally very strongly at the end: the surrender.
>
> Scherzo: main theme: called 'German Michel'.
>
> In the second part the lad wants to sleep, but in his dream he does not find his song. Finally complaining, lamenting, he reverses and turns the song around.
>
> Finale: In those days our Emperor received a visit from the Tsar in Ölmütz; thus strings: Ride of the Cossacks; Brass: military music, trumpets: fanfare as the royal majesties confront each other.
>
> Finally *all* themes as in Tannhäuser when the King comes in the second Act, so also when the 'German Michel' comes from his travels. In the finale there is also a 'Death march' and then 'transfiguration'.

The extract quoted here was regarded with great scepticism by research scholars as a document that could throw significant light on Bruckner's music.

In the meantime however it can be proved that Bruckner at least while composing the end-movements (1 and the finale) and the scherzo did actually start out with extra-musical imaginations and ideas which considerably influenced the gestalting of the music.

Stradal who found himself together with Bruckner in the train from Bayreuth kept a record of the encounter:

'Bruckner became very talkative, he spoke about his Eighth symphony, about the tolling of the bells for death, which has been imitated at the end of the first movement, about the "German Michel" who dances in scherzo, of the riding Cossacks at the meeting of the emperors of Austria and Russia; and of the powerful winds-theme, which is to introduce both the rulers.'

The First Movement and the Song of the Flying Dutchman

In his commentary to the first movement, Bruckner draws attention to the instances in the content which he designates as *Prophecy of Death* and *surrender/submission.*

A ten-time intonation of the dotted rhythm of the main theme in horns and trumpets; then the epilogue commences, the first motif taking up the main theme sounding in ppp. Here the concluding motif of the first theme is repeated.

Bruckner had designated this part as 'surrender' but also as 'Bells of Death': 'It is as when someone lies dying and opposite him hangs a clock, which while his life comes to an end always goes on ticking evenly—tick, tock, tick, tock . . .'

The inspiration for the composition of this movement came from the C–minor aria of the *Flying Dutchman.* As a result the main theme displays a marked similarity to the theme of this aria.

The intellectual relationship of the 'exegesis' of Bruckner and the text of the *Dutchman* aria is close. Bruckner talks about prophecy of Death and submission, the Dutchman sings about prophecy of Death, surrender, the Day of Judgment, and the resurrection of the dead. Even the finale of the symphony is related to Bruckner's programme, as we are going to see the 'Death march and transfiguration'.

The German Michel Scherzo

Bruckner told Weingartner that the Scherzo of the Eighth is a sort of portrait of the legendary gestalt of the 'German Michel'. The indication that this Michel may be 'Friend Almeroth' in Bruckner's sketches perhaps is a pointer to the possibility that in his friend Almeroth, Bruckner saw a personification of the German Michel.

The Scherzo is one of the most peculiar of Bruckner's compositions. It is constructed on three elementary motifs from which all themes and melodic lines are built. Bruckner said, 'He does not find his song'. In the music, vain attempts are made by the first flute to start. Only later does the complete Michel-theme appear in the flutes and the clarinets, but significantly in the reversal.

Bruckner's commentary helps to elicit and bring out the semantics of the three elementary motifs. He sketches the picture of the sleeping Michel, who is awakened and who then erects himself into his full size and steps on as a hero. In the middle part Bruckner sketches a magical picture of sleep into which Michel repeatedly sinks.

The trio has the following qualities of expression: the first period has a choral-like character, the second period shows a transformation into hymn-like ecstasy; the Romantic sound impression of the third period allows itself to be characterized as 'dreaming'.

Why does Bruckner select the gestalt of 'Michel' to be the subject matter of his Scherzo? For ages the German Michel has been the personification of the German essence and in the nineteenth century he became the political and folk symbol figure of Germanism. Hopes, disappointments and fears were bound with the Michel-figure: the hope for the founding of a German kingdom, the disappointments that came from the political lethargy of the German people, and finally the fear of being overcome in the political power games of the world powers. In the Austro-Hungarian monarchy, the German Michel was used to encourage the German population to be watchful against the Slavic people who were viewed with suspicion and mistrust as the 'inner enemies'. Bruckner dedicated the symphony to the Emperor and simultaneously related his work to an international political happening, the meeting of the Austrian emperor with the Tsar of Russia, thus expressing his patriotic feelings.

The Adagio

For several years religious-mystical interpretations and the programmatic interpretation of Joseph Schalk, who described the movement as 'the quiet hand of God: the all-loving father of men', were taken as standards.

Bruckner is supposed to have said the following about the first theme of this movement: 'Here I have looked too deeply into a maiden's eyes'. In connection with his introduction Schalk quoted most of the eight verses of the 'Prologue in Heaven' from the first part of *Faust*.

There are basically two theme complexes each working a fore- and an after-movement.

The first theme complex:	The fore-movement is oriented to the Tristan world: sighing-motif, motif of mourning, Death motif from Tristan—quotation from the Sad Shepherd tune. After-movement: contrasting: soaring ducts of the music, pure triads, hymnic conclusion with harp-sounds.
The second theme complex:	Fore-movement: ecclesiastical-liturgical (cantilena in the celli—Mozart's Requiem). After-movement: Tuba-chorale (Wagner and Grail idea). For the first time Bruckner uses Harps.

Finale

Bruckner's comments on the finale were never taken in earnest, perhaps because the *naiveté* of these comments appeared to be incompatible with the grand sublimity of the musical conception.

Over and above this, in no other final movement do approximately so many 'quotations' appear as do in this finale (the main theme of the first movement, motifs and rhythms of the remaining movements, retrospective survey flashbacks). Over here Bruckner apparently uses a technique which we know in the form of 'reminiscences' with the leit-motif.

The Finale also is surprising in other ways—through a series of peculiarities, which stand opposed to the criteria of the rules of composition. The borders between the exposition and the development are erased to such an extent that interpreters started the development at four different points. Bruckner's own comments are related to the beginning, the middle and the end of the finale. Bruckner claims the meeting between the emperor Franz Joseph I and the Tsar at Ölmütz as being the occasion for the creation of his symphony. Such a meeting did not take place in the period when the symphony was being composed. Bruckner perhaps was drawing upon the politically significant 'Meeting of three Emperors' (Emperor Wilhelm, Joseph I and the Tsar) in 1884.

1. *Theme-complex*
   Rhythm of the strings :
   His own theme :
   Trumpet fanfare :

Cossack ride
military music
Meeting of the rulers

The whole has the effect of a 'stage-music composition'.

2. *Theme-complex*
   Religious character (chorale-like) (Symbol of the Cross)

3. *Theme-complex*
   Death march
   Contrast : Theme of the death march is interrupted by choral-like ideas, later a synthesis through a further development into the flutes and pizzicatto strings.

Then : Winds intone the rhythm of the prophecy of Death from the first movement, while the drums, strings and bassoons hang on to the death march themes.

The 'Transformation' follows upon the death march. Horns play 'sighing' figures from the Adagio. Strings accompany in pizzicatto the rhythm of the death march theme.

The development contains elements from the 'sleeping' motif of the scherzo, death march and military music.

In the Reprise : Both the first parts of the main theme are repeated. Death march and choral-themes do not reappear.

In the Code : 'Apotheosis'. Astonishing skill in extending the whole structure into the gigantic, in that he breaks up, resolves the individual motifs and 'develops' these with transpositions.

One finds a sort of contrapuntal combination of all the main motifs simultaneously to this, the final *Appearance of the Michel motif.*

What is this diffuse arrangement meant to signify?

The arrangement of the different motifs points to or allows a very logical interpretation: the sleepy German Michel sleeps through decisive events in the Finale. These are however manifestations of the highest worldly powers (Meeting of the royal personages) and of the highest super-worldly instances (Death march—Transfiguration). The appearance of the Michel theme just before the end of the symphony probably means that the German Michel does really awaken from his deep sleep to be in time to participate in the end-result.

Allegro
allargando
a tempo
Moderato pesante

Mahler Interpretation

When avant-garde art is criticized for being unintelligible, and when it is suggested that this art must be universally understandable if it wishes to appeal to the masses, there lies in such an approach a very basic misunderstanding rooted in undialectical and unhistorical thinking. Everything that is labelled as being 'understandable to everybody' is mostly something which is not at all required to be understood. I would like to go further and claim that a 'new thought' that is understood rightaway is *not* a new thought. Or alternatively it is also possible that in order that this thought may be commonly understood it has been so formulated that it enters through one ear only to leave through the other. I would like to recall Adorno's substantiation for why a complex thought necessitates a complex language for its formulation and state that great works are within the grasp of the receiver but are also liable to be misunderstood by him. Or they only appear to have an aura of being easily understandable. Whoever understands a Mahler symphony at the first instance has already gone a long way towards misunderstanding it. But someone who is fascinated by the music without knowing the reasons why, will listen more carefully the next time, will reflect on the music and discover clues to aid an understanding of the work. Misunderstood Mahler is more difficult to repair than a Mahler who has not been understood. The misunderstanding hardens and sets, but the non-understanding leaves open the possibility that something may finally be understood. I would rather have Mahler unpopular than popular for the wrong reasons. To discover where these wrong reasons lie one does not have to seek long. The greatest number of the performances and recordings responsible for influencing the reception of Mahler's work, are performances which bring his music down to a mediocre level. These performances subtract from the aggressive element in the music and make it commercial, i.e. the music is served as an appetizing morsel, making it easily accessible and at the same time also incomprehensible. Now, this matter of Misunderstanding and Non-understanding however, does not allow itself to be transferred in an analogous or parallel way on to the person responsible for the performances of Mahlerian music. It is indeed possible to separate the majority of the interpreters into those who understand Mahler, and those who either do not understand him at all, or do not wish to understand him. But, from the point of view of the result and audience-reception (and this is the crux of the matter), it appears that the interpreters or conductors who have *not* understood Mahler at all, in the end-effect, cause a greater confusion in the listener than is caused by the interpreters who have misunderstood him. Let us assume that there are conductors for whom music is principally a vehicle of self-projection—these are mostly the 'Stars', and there are others who also desire to communicate something of and from the work itself. In such a case, the latter group of interpreters (assuming that Mis-understanding does not reign total) will at least partially deliver matter for discussion and reflection. The non-understanding interpretation would not awaken any curiosity or any desire to find out more about the work.

The following incident appears to me to be symptomatic of the problem. While leaving the hall after a performance of the Second Symphony conducted by Bernstein in Bonn, I could not avoid listening to how a young woman nearby raved in loud and ecstatic tones about Bernstein's conducting. I was somewhat consoled when one of her companions asked her how she had liked the symphony and she answered half-proudly, half-condescendingly, 'Oh, I did not notice it all'. This comment not only corroborated my estimation of Bernstein's Mahler-interpretation and its effect, I also thought to myself that not listening is better than listening incorrectly. Of course, one may not generalize about a whole audience in such a way, and certainly on that evening there was a broad spectrum between mis-understanding and non-understanding—and definitely even some who had also listened critically. Stravinsky once wrote an article entitled *How One Should not Play Beethoven's Sonatas*. It was an important contribution to the subject of interpretation. However, if I were to go into how one should not play Mahler (examples for which exist in plenty), there would be no putting an end to the topic. I would prefer to tackle the problems that Mahler poses in a performance, problems on which even the best intentioned run aground.

Take the third movement of the First Symphony which on first sight appears to be very simple, and even conductors, who are wholly unacquainted with Mahler, very rarely succeed in making a complete hash of it. Yet even in the best of performances the impression left behind is unsatisfactory. Let us consider the first part movement—the Frere-Jacques Canon—and concentrate on the problems. The first relates to the contra-bass solo at the start of movement. In order to understand what Mahler intended here it is very important—more important than it is with Bach and Monteverdi—to take into consideration the state of the playing technique at the time this work was composed. In the music composed up to that time not much was required of the contra-bass player; his part was mostly a duplication of the cello part. He merely provided the sonic foundation. He did not need to possess any technique nor was he required to play any melodies. The fact that Mahler entrusted the exposition of the theme to such an instrument has something to do with the fact that given the existing conditions the theme was not expected to be played perfectly, that it would sound uncultivated and awkward, almost a little as if the music were emanating from a pub or a bar in the distance. This effect is lost, when the players today concentrate on giving their best. One can sympathize with this desire to make their best of it, for the contra-bassists are seldom given an opportunity to play such an important theme. In reality they are the most underprivileged in the whole orchestra. The conductor must therefore convince the first contra-bassist that he has to shine not through excellent playing but through characteristic playing—not to produce a beautiful sound, but a grotesque one—and to smudge the legato a little bit.

One could perhaps say that the Fifth Symphony presents fewer problems, that in this case it is possible to interpret directly from the score, and that it does not contain as many ambivalent elements as do the Seventh, Fourth or the Third symphonies. Yet it is essential to concentrate on a simple, clear and slender sound. Instead of this however this work mostly dissolves into a broadness—the quality of the sound as well as the course of the music—and the tempi become slower from year to year. Where in Bruno Walter's recording of 1947 the symphony had once lasted sixty minutes—and he was not an especially stormy conductor—the total time taken by today's recordings can be anything from 68 to 81 minutes. The worst effect of this broad cinemascope pathos is to be seen on poor ill-treated Adagietto, the character and function of which in the context of the whole is not difficult to recognize. It is not to be regarded as a Brucknerian Adagio movement, but is to be treated as a weighty interlude or maybe even as a prelude to the Finale, with which it forms a unit; the diminutive form of the term Adagietto is an adequate indication and clue of this. Yet our conductors waltz out this movement as if they fancied themselves on the sets of a Visconti film.

No other symphony is so drastically played and sung with a complete disregard for the original score as is the Eighth. It is really no wonder that the conductor when first confronted with the silly sub-title 'The Symphony of the Thousand', the invention of a business-minded impresario, thinks that the more senselessly the choir shouts into the space, the better the piece will function, and that therefore they will be relieved of the responsibility of reflecting on the problems of interpretation. The exegetic researchers on Mahler have not been of much help so far. On the contrary, they have added to the general confusion because they have, as if on principle, disregarded the text and what Mahler made out of it.

It is not possible to understand the Eighth by examining the score alone. Although Hans Mayer, who (in his article about Mahler's relationship to literature) declared that the link between the Pentecostal hymn and the conclusion of *Faust II*, to be one which does not hold, he could have discovered from the score that this link is not only legitimate, but above all, one which makes sense, because the parallels that Mahler discovered in the text are underlined with parallel motifs and themes. But mostly it is the other way round. One arrives at the meaning of the score through the words, or more precisely through the manner in which Mahler handles the words. For example, one discovers that the two lines of the Pentecostal hymn must have had a very central significance for Mahler: the lines 'accende lumen sensibus' (kindle light to the senses) and the concluding 'Infunde amorem cordibus' (Administer love to the hearts).

How then does Mahler make clear that these two lines especially were of vital importance to him, that they were decisive for his choice of material? It shows in the fact that Mahler remains extendedly with these two lines; and indeed in a drawn out part with solo voices and again in a tender, transparent instrumental part; then when the music changes its key, its dynamics and its character, and one expectantly awaits the transition into the next section, Mahler returns anew to the 'accende lumen'. It is no candle that is lit over here, instead a volcano erupts. Yet when you hear this part on the record you will wonder: 'Where is the volcano?'—and you may well wonder because all that one now hears is an undifferentiated fortissimono, a tutti with all the choirs including a children's. In the score however, there is more to be discovered. Mahler tears the word 'accende' apart: the first syllable 'ac' is intoned briefly, broken off, a short pause ensues and it is on the 'cende' that the eruption follows. This could be one of the breathtaking moments in music if only it were performed as Mahler had conceived of it. But this breathing space is totally disregarded or excessively shortened, and then one can no longer think of volcanoes, especially when it is followed up by an undifferentiated fortissimo in which the vocal polyphony is more or less drowned.

In contrast to this however, Rafael Kubelik at least observes this breathing space in his recording of the work; only he makes it rather too brief, so that the intended effect is not achieved. But in the following part he does come somewhat closer to Mahler than do other conductors. The choir does not merely shout, but also makes an effort to articulate music and text: and unadulterated volume is replaced by sharply accentuated and tensely energetic recitation.

Understanding Mahler's Third Symphony

1

Gustav Mahler began the composition of his Third Symphony in the summer of 1895, at the age of thirty-five, after preparatory work. He completed it a year later on 5 August 1896 in Steinbach on Attersee. He wrote the gigantic Symphony, one of the largest in existence, within the short period of two working summers. (Except on holidays, Mahler could barely get down to the task of composing because of his commitments as a conductor.) Individual movements of the work were performed in early 1897. The complete symphony was premièred six years later in 1902 in Krefeld. It was a great success, but not an undisputed one to be sure; and the way to this achievement had been a long and difficult one.

Mahler came from simple circumstances; his beginnings were in the country. The small Bohemian Jew did not find it easy to work his way up. Like his fellow-countryman Freud, he too had to suffer all his life under the taint of his Jewish descent. Feeling the pressure of the material circumstances, which he had to bear in addition to the burden of belonging to a defamed folk, Mahler reacted very early to the uncertainty of the circumstances, exposing a greater vulnerability than a person belonging to a renowned family in a big city would have done. He wrote his first symphonies and the *Wunderhornlieder* ('magic horn songs') in the late eighties and early nineties which was a time of prosperity. Bourgeois capitalism, and connected with it, national imperialism, celebrated triumphs which led to considerable prosperity among the upper classes and the upper-middle classes, and it did seem as though these rosy days were going to last. Yet Mahler's music more appropriately approaches and expresses the feelings and emotions bound with our present-day conditions than his own times. These break out particularly in the more modern parts. Unlike the Straussian boldness, which rises either from the need for illustration or from a quasi-technological progressive thinking, the bold sections in Mahler are based on expression. His penetrating sounds, the dissonant instrumental parts and even his unusual polyphony express that all is not as harmonious as it appears to be. In this expression, the latent instability of the late-bourgeois conditions are registered and reflected. In some cases this reflection is really drastic. When in 1893, a concentrated process of rearmament had been in progress in Germany (the first signs of a crisis which broke out twenty years later in the shape of the First World War), this aggressive rearmament, this threatening clanking of sabres, found an almost prophetic portrayal in the chaotic passages of the Third Symphony, particularly towards the end of the first movement with its percussion noise. Mahler himself was instinctively on the side of the proletariat, on the side of those who had received nothing from the prosperity. In their choice of text, the *Wunderhornlieder* already showed a deviation from all that was the norm in those days. Instead of the lyrics of bourgeois individualism, folk songs were taken over word for word from the members of the lower levels of society—soldiers, poor people from the country, wandering performers, gypsies and prisoners. The tone of these texts recalls Brecht occasionally, and their contents are considerably sharpened when set to music by Mahler. In the song 'The Earthly Life', the naked need of the hungry people is made to cry out accusingly; 'The Song of the Persecuted Man in Prison' is the protest-song of a prisoner, and in 'Where the Beautiful Trumpets Sound' the theme is the senselessness of war. The purely instrumental third movement of the Third Symphony speaks the same language as those songs. Perhaps it is this hidden political aspect of Mahler's music which puts his sparing and limited success in an ambivalent light; and which causes concealed uneasiness even today.

That Mahler wished to speak in this manner, i.e. in 'folk tone' really, is explained by the fact that he himself spoke the language of the lower folk; to him it was something like a mother-tongue. Unlike Strauss and most of his other contemporaries, Mahler assimilated the musical culture from below, from the side that was associated with poverty. Folk music was what he came to learn and know well, before coming in contact with any other kind of music. Folk music belonging to the lower levels of society, to the countryside which also nourished the music of the urban proletariat songs, included chorals, dance-music for the simplest ensembles consisting of brass-winds, plucked string instruments, concertinas and other similar instruments. Moreover, in Bohemia, this folk music was more strongly rooted in genuine folklore than it was in Germany and Austria. Simultaneously in those early years, the then omnipresent military music infiltrated to Mahler in his home-town and left its impression behind. It was only after this that Mahler came in touch with bourgeois music—classical music, opera, as well as the higher level of entertainment music played on social occasions. Mahler quite sensibly adapted himself quickly to this music, and during his studies with the old-fashioned Bruckner he also acquainted himself with the rules of archaic-counterpoint and church music. Mahler never repudiated what was to an extent the proletariat past of his musical language. Mahler's music is differentiated from that of his contemporaries in the multifacetedness of its language: it does not move in a single, lingual field but in several. His sympathies do not just speak the highly developed language of classical music, as is otherwise usual, but they also converse in the dialects of folk music, as well as in the coarse, uncultivated language of what is termed 'trivial music'. This incorporation of several strains as well as lower music forms by preference makes Mahler's music appear heterogeneous, flat and lacking in style. His music agitated the critics of his time and also such reasonable and understanding colleagues as Schönberg. Even today, on occasions, his music is faulted for triviality, for lacking in originality and for having disjointed sequences. In the Third Symphony this multilinguality is expounded bluntly and almost provokingly. Each of the six movements speaks its own musical language. The first movement speaks at first the jargon of military music and then incorporates the somewhat more elevated language of funeral marchers. The second movement plays the classical music of the bourgeois concert hall. The minuet-character of this piece lends it a slightly antiquated tone viewed with a certain amount of nostalgia—as a contrast the musical language of ball-rooms is also heard in places—as in the instance where a Polka is quoted. The third movement presents the music of the lower classes—poor people's music, so to speak. This is emphasized right at the beginning not only by the simple construction, but also through the choice of instruments—pizzicatti from plucked string instruments, clarinets, pipes (namely piccolo-flutes), and finally the brass-music of the trumpets. At two points as if visually faded in parts, a post-horn sounds—the music of times gone by. The fourth movement conjures up the idiom of church music and of a folk music akin to it. In the fifth movement Mahler quotes the musical language of children in its strong pentatonically coloured melody. The final movement stands in between the spheres of all the languages. It speaks a non-elite musical language encompassing that which qualifies as 'high' and that which qualifies as 'low' both in the same degree. Moreover, the source-material for the six movements are, traditionally speaking, themes which are closely related to one another. The horn signal, placed at the beginning of the symphony like a motto the start of which, in addition, quotes the song 'Ich hab mich ergeben' almost word for word, emphasizes an ascending and descending quart-interval. This quart construction serves to alienate the melody of the song and obscures the tonality. It swings between D-minor and B-major. The quart forms the germ cell of all the other themes. The theme of the second movement is locked by two quarts at both ends of it. In the third movement the theme circles around the quint and the quart, which behave as complements to each other. The fourth movement verticalizes, at first without a theme, the intervals of sound. In the different theme a material kern of quarts is spun out every time.

This precisely is then the formal idea of a symphony, the unfolding of a thing in new directions. Mahler has divided the work into two parts. The first comprises of the huge 40 minute long first movement; after which, according to a remark in the first edition of the score, a pause of five minutes is to follow. The remaining five movements form the second part lasting over an hour. The first movement, i.e. the first part, has a dynamic, purposeful character, as it portrays a powerful development. The remaining five movements, comprising the second part, are less purposefully ordered. Each of them is a complete piece of music resting upon itself and no movement presses towards the other.

In a programme (which he did not publish himself, but which he had communicated to an acquaintance in a letter), Mahler symbolically formulated the curious, unsymphonic, suitelike arrangement of the work and its serial order. Unfortunately this formulation appears very often in interpretations of the symphony and in concert programme notes, where it causes considerable damage. It makes a private elucidation of Mahler binding on the listener and directs his powers of association in a specific direction. This is limiting because in truth the field of possible associations the music can evoke is multivalent and incomparably larger. The programme is one from which, as Mahler so cautiously puts it, one may perhaps find a small sign to guide the way, as follows:

Part I
Introduction—Pan awakes
No. 1 The Summer marches in
Part II
No. 2 What the flowers on the meadows say to me
No. 3 What the beasts in the forests say to me
No. 4 What Man says to me
No. 5 What the Angels say to me
No. 6 What Love says to me[1]

When one looks away from the Jugendstil-like, if not almost 'kitsch'-ish associations in 'Summer's entry', 'Flowers on the meadow', 'Beasts in the Forests', 'Man', 'Angels', 'Love', then a directional process is visualized for the first part, awakening and marching in a specific direction; while the movements in the second part are non-directional, practically vegetative events, narrations, placed next to each other. Therefore, the form of the symphony is so arranged that out of the dynamic happenings of the first movement, the more static events of the following movements should diverge more or less radically as if from the grip of a central hub. One could almost wish for a spatially arranged performance of this symphony which at any rate has been conceived as such. In such a performance, after the performance of the first part in a central chamber, the performance of the remaining movements could take place in separate rooms arranged around this chamber. The form of the symphony in its second part is definitely not exclusively centrifugal. The last movement folds together once more the units that had been spread out, which could have been concentrated into a unity again, only after the richness of the piece had been unfolded. The Third Symphony is Mahler's optimistic piece. Perhaps this optimism reflects his personal experiences from the time of Mahler's great successes, and the general mood of everything right with the world has been captured by him. The glorious period of these years would also have generated high spirits in Mahler. The simultaneous strengthening of the progressive forces in the society would have strengthened the hope for better times. Thus Mahler's Third Symphony became his great Utopia. This Utopia is sketched out methodically in the first movement and then described part by part in the other movements till it finally finds completion in the Finale. In the idiom of his times and with the help of its ideas Mahler said in a letter that the Third is 'a musical poem encompassing all the stages of development in ascending steps. It begins with sleeping Nature and escalates itself to the Love of God.' An introduction precedes the first movement but the progress from the one to the other is without a break. In the programme mentioned before, the introduction is called 'Pan awakes', and if Mahler, in a letter, speaks of the beginning as an awakening from an apathetic, rigid, merely elementary existence of Nature, then the introduction constitutes the event of the beginning, where the things gradually get into a movement and go over from a state of disorder and formlessness, into a state of form poised to acquire life.

The horns open the symphony with the already mentioned motto—a motto of optimism. The sound then recedes, as the accords that recall church music and begin the Fifth Symphony, appear. Out of a blurred percussion roll, the rhythm of a funeral march develops, but it does not acquire the right form. A figure in the bassoon, a 'calling motif' in the woodwinds, a sharp trumpet signal and wild interrupting phrases in the deep strings are repeated in a disorderly way. This chaotic situation intensifies itself when, after some time, the horns attempt to articulate something resembling a melody. This attempt goes on for a long time but does not have any success. The quasi-melody collapses into itself and disappears into an indistinct percussion roll. Woodwind chords then sound, but only to be wiped out by a whirring string-tremolo. Soon another nice melody appears—played by the oboe and the solo violin—a new attempt to build forms, one which also points forward to the fifth movement (with children's music), the violin solo presaging the second movement. This attempt is destroyed by the interruption of the shrieking clarinets. The poor music made by these clarinets is later developed in the third movement—at present it leads to nothing but is lost in the characteristic sound of the deep strings and disappears into the percussion. Simple rhythms in the percussion bring the introduction to an end. In this music, barely developed, with its manifold hints of what is to come, the terrain in which the symphony and its utopia unfold is identified.

The actual first movement consists of three sections, each with two or three smaller parts, reminiscent of the old sonata scheme: exposition, development and reprise. The proportions are indeed over-dimensional and the individual parts form building blocks which are in themselves almost complete units, like independent movements which are only loosely connected with one another, with hardly any connecting passages. In the first section there is a part which corresponds to the main movement with the first theme—a whole funeral march, or rather, a unit similar to a funeral march. The essence of this is formed by a gigantic trombone solo with an almost prose-like rhythm. It takes up the rudimentary melody played by the horns in the introduction and transforms it into a forcefully articulated music of the highest expressive quality. The inarticulate stammering heard earlier changes into a free speech of great tone and large gesture. Towards the end it becomes urging, almost wild, and acquires the character of protest and agitation.

A march complex follows a quasi-secondary movement with the second theme—or what may sooner be termed a second real main movement. Out of a march-rhythm, at first indistinct but gradually acquiring precision, new march melodies keep appearing, in which the motto, now with the no longer alienated folk-song quotation, plays a special role. The tone of this march music is bright, almost cheerful; but the richly used small drums and other percussion instruments give it a peculiar sharpness, making it appear military. Here one is marching, and indeed—forward. The whole march complex is a uniquely long, extended escalation, and the climax is dissonantly loud and explosive. Out of this climax a big prose melody, which had made up the first complex, i.e. the quasi-main movement one, breaks out abruptly. This time it is not played by the solo-trombone alone, but by all the brasswinds; and it has in addition an animated tempo which results in the expression becoming uncontrolled, screaming as if in panic, till the strong excitement subsides and the solo-trombone continues the melody alone, sentimental and resigned; only to be finally taken up by the English-horn when it sounds plaintive and forlorn. That is the first part of the second section—traditionally speaking, the development. This section has three parts. The second part is idyllic, full of natural sounds, scurrying trills, calling figures and chirruping of birds. Its quiet climax is a duo between the horn and the solo violin, in the ecstatic beauty of which the music becomes quiet. This symbolizes a retreat into lonely regions, inwards. In this moment of quiet, the march complex makes a raw intrusion. It starts directly in forte, and in the way the prose melody complex had broken out in panic and regressive anxiety before, the march complex now breaks out into unconcealed aggressiveness. In its construction, the third part of the second section is of raw, uncultivated simplicity on the one side, and demonstrates chaotic complexity on the other. Here, Mahler composes a polyphony which was to foreshadow a more modern composer, Ives. In this polyphony, several kinds of music, each having its own character, tonality and tempo, are piled up one upon another so that a polytonal and polyrhythmic structure results. The furious aggression is crushed to an extent. A drum signal is blended into its shadow disappearance, and this signal flows out into the motto. The sweeping resumption of the motto marks the start of the third section, i.e. the reprise. In its first part the trombone sole returns, but with a great quietness and without the escalation that had been present before. Instead, there is a very solemn passage in piano which is played to the end in the warm tones of the violoncello. This time, therefore, the trombone solo does not have its rousing and protesting tone, but expresses complaints, and in its quieter phases, consolation.

The quiet reprise of the march complex, the second part of the third section, which follows now, appears different. The use of the small drums that had clanked so incessantly in the first march phase, is considerably reduced here—a small, but significant difference which takes away from the march complex its military sharpness. The tone is bright and relaxed; the swing however has a transporting and stirring quality, which would like to carry everyone in its flow. This all-encompassing quality expresses itself in the part of the movement which is the richest harmonically and melodically. Mahler superscribed it thus—'with great expression'. The warm sound and embracing gesture are expressions of reconciliation. This is why this part is taken up once more in the final movement where the theme is love, and indeed, love among all mankind. Following the pause in this expressive moment, the escalation climbs higher, till in a great climax it leads to the finale with loud jubilation.

The course of the movement is as follows: rousing speech in Part I of Section I; aggressive march with a dissonant climax in Part II; panic screams and paralysis in Part I of Section II, retreat into silence in Part II, section II; aggressive marches of an overthrowing nature, ending in a big fanfare in Part III, Section II; plaintive, consoling speech in Part I, section III; cheerful, all-encompassing march ending in rejoicing in Part II, Section III. Is the liberation of mankind being expressed here? Is Society being summoned to overthrow the prevailing order and open up at last to a new future and age? It cannot prove anything, because the language of music is equivocal. And yet, what speaks here is an immediate language of direct expression. In any case, in this huge movement Mahler's Utopia deals with liberation.

2

The five movements of the Second Part deal with the consequence of Mahler's Utopia—with freedom. Freedom as a realization of Mahler's Utopia demands that every means of expression and every language should come into its own right. Therefore the variety and diversity of the musical languages and their richness of expression is pointed out. Taboo languages are liberated from the bans on them. Where the language frees itself it acquires an eloquent narrative quality. A theme is touched upon, spun out and developed, a secondary thought is introduced and from there it proceeds in quite a different direction; so that the narrative is uninterrupted and does not lose any threads, but these threads curl into new patterns and roll in different directions. So these five movements have a rare formless something—signs of freedom, a freedom where a language can dare to unfold itself.

Mahler called the second movement, in which the classical music and music allied to it, e.g. the music of bells, is developed, his flower piece. In actuality the sound blossoms over here—so the solo woodwinds, harps and strings play the minuet in a chamber-music fashion for a while. An accordic sound base is then built by the horns, flutes and the trumpets, which moreover changes to a sound colour melody the moment the music, tenderly sketched so long, starts to glow colourfully. A similar thing happens when the horizontal melody is surrounded by instrumental ornamentation and to a certain extent form tendrils around themselves. This piece, therefore, has something Nature-like despite its highly differentiated and precious language, in that the sound always creates new blossoms. It speaks the language of the lyrical subject, which takes up the beauty of the thing feelingly and lets it find a linguistic form. Opposed to this the play of the third movement is undifferentiated. Its simple music has clear, almost coarsely drawn contours. Here speaks the language of the collective subject, that of the folk, more specifically, the idiom of the lower classes. The idiom is spun out to bring a great wealth of characters to light. At times the music becomes pitiful and begins to lament, at other times it turns defiant and starts to grumble, at certain points it sinks into a tone of sentimentality, at others it breaks out in anger and acquires something shrieking and ordinary. All this, in which many kinds of folk music, or the music of the lower classes, is captured, sounds like brass bands, barrel organs and street ballads, like village dance halls but also like sentimental songs. At two places there appears a post-horn melody, which sings of the good old times. The lower music therefore becomes eloquent and indeed in a different way from the upper, in that it expresses without constraint and shame and with every precision, how an individual and a society feel. Consequently Mahler lets this language flow unhindered. He uses new composition techniques. Instead of binding different musical courses with linking bridges, he allows one to run on and blends the second in gradually, e.g. the post-horn part which is already at hand long before its actual appearance, and again, in its sound a new course is played in. In this composition technique, not used for the lower music just by chance, Mahler realizes his idea of polyphony. A Mahler anecdote runs: 'On a Sunday as we went with Mahler along the same way a witches' Sabbath was on in the festival at Kreuzberg. There were uncountable swings, merry-go-rounds, shooting galleries and puppet shows along with military music and a male voice choral society. On the same meadow, regardless of each other they were creating an unbelievable music, when Mahler cried: "Do you hear that? That is Polyphony. It is from there that I have it. Exactly so must the themes come from different sides and so fully undifferentiated should they be in rhythm and melody (all other polyphony is plain multivoicedness and disguised homophony)".'[2] One may also add that this is the colourful and multiformed polyphony of life itself, an effect that John Cage was to seek later. The fourth movement moves in the sphere of religious music. Appropriate to its character as an art which is connected with words, an alto solo is included here. The text is a poem from Nietzsche's *Zarathustra.* After the introduction where the 'O Man, take care' sounds out of the archaic accords as out of the depths, the music unfolds a long, sustained, surging, pulsating sound (D–A). To it the brass-winds intone partly choral and partly calling phrases, a long, still music practically of reverberating silence, almost recalling a La Monte Young meditative phase. The words are: 'What does the deep midnight speak? I slept! I slept! Out of a deep dream I've been awakened! The World is deep, and thought of deeper as the day!' An instrumental interlude follows it. In it the individual parts of the choral phrases melt into a wide, gripping, speaking melody. The religious idiom is freed from the old-fashioned rigidity. The music then seems to sink into the depths and the call, 'O Man, take care,' sounds a second time. In the second meditative phase following upon it the sustenato goes quickly into vibration. In the place of the winds with its choral impressions the solo violin now plays tender and sensitive melodies of immediate, speaking expression. The religious language becomes completely individual. The words deal with pain in the world: 'Deep is her woe! Desire deeper as heartache! Woe speaks—pass away!' Such pain has been taken up deep in its own feeling. At the concluding words, 'Yet all desire wants Eternity', the music begins to flow and to glow. The solo melody goes into the common warmly flowing sound. After the religious music itself has become free it is able to encompass each individuality. What it symbolically expresses here is how desire in the depth of the world pushes towards and transforms all, encompassing them to Eternity. In Mahler's Utopia the musical formulation becomes the religious herald of a new time.

If this music is played in the loneliness of introversion, the fifth movement plays in the extroverted communal sphere where one goes out of oneself. The movement is for a boys' choir placed in an elevated position, a women's choir (as usual behind the orchestra) and an altoist standing in front, a highly theatrical performance. The text is one of the infantile *wunderhorn* poems. In reality it brings to the music continually new forms of dramatic invention, as invented during play, even as it unfolds the field of childish speech. There are pathetic recitations placed against cheerful rhymes, or fretful declamations, which are calmed with verses spoken so as to muffle the effect, and the almost monotonous repetition of the always present 'Bim-bam'. Here is touched, not only the plaintive plea for compassion and the childish guilt feeling of a bad conscience, but one also hears chiding words, commands and the voice of consolation. The music created from the funds of children's songs is not exclusively bright, but at times it is peculiarly sharp and threatening; as the child-like sensibility that remains in the depth of adults is not just cheerful but mixed with dark shudders. However this children's piece has a good end: 'The heavenly joy is a blissful city, the heavenly joy that has no end.'

The greatness of Mahler's Utopia lies in the fact that the Utopia is not portrayed as an insipid, conflict-free state, but as one with a wealth of possibilities. It is an unfolding pure and simple, which in no way progresses without conflicts and dark phases, but actually comes into existence in the overcoming of conflicts. Mahler expressed this musically so that in the individual movements of the second part, he could intentionally incorporate all forms of expression that exist and did this without contempt. He could bring together the differing language spheres of the cultural 'high' language, the 'folk' language of communication, the language of mature sensibility and the language of children playing. They all express themselves, everything is spoken about, even silence has its right. Mahler's music is the language of reconciliation, as it encompasses everything to finally become the language of love. It sounds in the finale of Mahler's symphony as pure music, without words. The long, slow movement is a simple, many-dimensional melody, or, differently expressed, a single, welling, pulsating sound current, which changes continually, constantly building new forms and yet remaining the same; one which swells and begins to surge, softens again and yet maintains its directions. The theme of the movement, or better the figure with which it begins, is a variation of the motto at the beginning of the symphony. Here it has shed the fanfarelike, fighting shape and appears in its reconciliatory form. The music growing out of this does not remain permanently warm and in Major. Repeatedly it changes to a bare music reduced to Minor, where the sensitivity contracts, so to speak, and sadness takes its place. But likewise this melancholic music dissolves into the warmth, which wins a richer form each time. So this music of reconciliation becomes a process of tension and release which leads further and further. The music which Mahler fittingly entitled 'What love says to me' describes its form, and forms. If at first it speaks more generally of love, of common love, so it also incorporates in increasing measure the tone of eroticism, as it is found in Wagner's *Tristan*. In the last phase of the movement, part of the movement which signified encompassing reconciliation is taken up again. Here it sounds rather more individual like a love between two. The hope that such a thing may also be possible undisturbed and unhindered is expressed: individuality and generality thus merge into a Unity. The movement, and with it Mahler's great Utopia, ends simply: in long, bright, 'D' major sounds of a saturated noble tone, with the sound of a satisfaction that prophesies genuine satiation.

1 Alma Mahler, *Gustav Mahler*: *Memories and Letters*, London 1968.
2 Henri-Louis de la Grange, *Mahler*, London 1974.

Mahler's Influence on Film Music

The question whether or not Mahler influenced film music cannot be answered directly. More carefully formulated, the question may be put as follows: Are there points of contact between the works and the personality of Gustav Mahler on one side and film music, or more specifically, certain types of film music and personalities representing them, on the other? Our question is: did Gustav Mahler himself compose film music? Not that we know of, but we become aware of the possibility that he might have done so. The earliest film music in the modern sense, i.e. the first accompanying music which was created for the concerti requirements of a specific film, already existed in 1908, a couple of years before Mahler's death. It was the work of a composer, who like Mahler, came from the concert hall and enjoyed as great a reputation there as Mahler did, namely Camille Saint-Saens. The film is a historical one-actor presentation of the French company, Film d'art, and was entitled *The Assassination of the Duke of Guise.*

It took more than half a century to form the definitive genre we call today Film Music. The formative period was between 1910–1960. During these years Film Music oriented towards models of an autonomous form. This sort of orientation was codified as early as 1907, when the first collection of accompanying pieces for the silent film pianists was brought on the market by the biggest American film company at the time, The Edison Company. Like its countless successors this collection was based on a clear principle. It had at the beginning an index of headings in which the typical film situations were listed under 'labels'. This was followed by a piano album which offered suggestions for the incidental music to these situations. The pianist was put in a position where he had to complete a sort of piano arrangement for each film that he had to accompany. It was a so-called 'cue-sheet'. On the left side of the sheet were given the visual cues to the events and on the right side the selected pieces, and variations on these which he was often compelled to play from several considerations. The modulatory course of the connecting passages with which he had to combine the individual numbers into a pauseless continual suite were also noted. The repertoire of such collections at first consisted of romantic 'character pieces' —Mendelssohn's 'Songs without Words', some Schumann, Grieg, Jensen, Chopin (a few Nocturnes, to start with), and even Rachmaninoff. The repertoire also made use of original compositions by authors who are almost forgotten today (Wilson, Zanecnik, Largey). Since these original compositions had to be attached to suites, they had to be compatible. They therefore had to be written in the style of the 'character pieces', which meant mostly that single thematic ideas were built up into simple song-like structures.

The importance of Kinotheks

The film music sound changed from that of the piano to that of the orchestra approximately around the time of the First World War. The Nickelodeons were replaced by large cinema theatres and première palaces, as the trend towards luxury spread. In this phase of the silent film the largest cinema orchestra had up to eighty members. As far as possible these orchestras were equipped in the pattern of the symphony orchestra. Soon the orchestra conductor took over the function which formerly belonged to the 'cue-sheet' pianist. And as the pianist had relied upon his piano the conductor was chiefly dependent upon what the 'Kinothek' had to offer. One must think of these 'Kinotheks', the first of which was opened in 1919 in Berlin by Giuseppe Becce, as gigantic archives, in which a countless number of short orchestral pieces were catalogued in an index of their contents. The conductor had at his disposal an index of headings in the form of a catalogue listing the beginnings. He saw the films that he had to underscore, one or two times. He noted the types of the scenes and their approximate length. He then sought out the fitting music in the catalogue and called for the different parts and the score. He was then required to arrange it, on one side according to the exact length of the scene and on the other to match the instrumental composition of his orchestra. As the pianist had done before him, the conductor combined the pieces with connecting bridge passages to accompany the film without a break. These 'Kinotheks' were fed from three different sources. At first, they acquired the apocryphal orchestral arrangements of the most favourite 'character pieces', those which had ornamented the 'cue-sheet' collections before. The second source were of almost unrecognizably simplified extracts from operas reduced virtually to 'character pieces', the operas ranging from Massenet to Puccini via Wagner. The third source was of original compositions, again by composers forgotten today (Becce, Erdmann, Leuchner), who out of the need for compatibility aimed at achieving the quality and style of the orchestral 'character pieces'. Going with some caution, one can characterize the style of the Kinothek music in terms of monothematic, songlike basic structures and sequences that may be omitted as main voice. Finally in view of the whole development, there emerged a 'sound picture', albeit a 'sound' that belongs somewhere between Tchaikovsky, Strauss and Rachmaninoff.

Film music in the Sound Era

Film music changed its point of reference as it changed from 'character pieces' to the symphonic principle, roughly with the beginning of the sound era. At the root of this change were profound and incisive technical and practical changes. In the silent film the music was compiled from simple numbers of the most differing kinds and played 'live' during each performance by the pianist, and later by the orchestra. In the sound film the music was, as a rule, composed by one individual composer for the demands of a specific film, recorded in the studio with the pictures and technically fixed to the film once and for all. This really gave the composer the chance to concern himself more closely with the visual events. He was no longer required to underscore, simply as an additive, but could take up details of the visual happenings, reflect them or simply carry them over. For the moment, the composers seized the chance and indeed landed often enough in sheer tautology. On the other hand even when they did become tautological, they freed the sound of film music. Now the eight-bar periodized melody and the limited 'character piece' form stood in their way. They started to take up open themes, turned to short contrasting motifs, which they could blend into each other, vary, work together contrapuntally, build up or liquefy. The label 'symphonic' may aptly be applied to these methods of creating film music.

The symphonic Hollywood style was inaugurated by a composer who came from Vienna. Born in 1888, Max Steiner was said to have been a student at first of Robert Fuchs and then of Gustav Mahler. The question of the authenticity of this statement is a delicate one in that the possibility that Mahler knew the apparently highly gifted young theatre conductor Steiner and even advised him in a couple of cases, is not to be rejected outright. Be that as it may, the first peak of the symphonic style was achieved by a musician, who as a wonderchild composer was the protégé of Gustav Mahler: Erich Wolfgang Korngold. One knows that in 1909 Mahler urged the twelve year old Korngold to give up his studies with Robert Fuchs and to go to Alexander von Zemlinsky. Zemlinsky thought so highly of Korngold that he orchestrated his pantomime 'The Snowman', the work of an eleven year old.

With its orientation towards the symphonic principle, film music reached the point at which influences from Mahler could have penetrated into it. Both the most influential representatives of the early Hollywood symphony had had definite connections with Mahler in their youth. Had they, a good twenty years later, taken up characteristics of Mahler's composition and used them in the service of the film?

The attention of a film music specialist is drawn to two things in Mahler's work, which I would like to assume are the ones to be blamed for Mahler's creative activity being denounced over the generations as partly tasteless, if not vulgar.

Firstly, in Mahler parts recur, in which the polyphony, in use from the time of Beethoven, polarizes to a sort of gesticulatory homophony, resulting in all the voices concerned giving a sort of profile to a single, clear and pronounced gesture.

Furthermore, there are in Mahler parts which occur repeatedly in which appear 'reserved materials' in the psychoanalytical sense of the term. These are materials which through decades, generations, epochs, if not centuries, have become precisely fixed on their contents of associations. Indeed so precise are their suggestive powers, that the listener is momentarily awakened to a definite sphere of associated images. It must be remembered that gesticulatory homophony and the mood created with 'reserved material'—with clichés, if you like—are the most important mood-creating devices in the experience of film music.

It would be precipitate to conclude at this point that the proof of Mahler's influence on film music has been provided. The conditions in which we receive film music are very different from those in which we receive pure non-filmic music. As a rule we do not go to the movies to listen to the music, but allow ourselves to be told a story. And this story is almost always created or told so as to touch us on three levels. The first is in the psychological field as we get to see more in a film than we do in everyday life. Secondly it is on the intellectual level as we must construct for ourselves a continuous story out of the mosaic-like presentation in disembodied situations. Thirdly on the psychological plane, the stories that we are offered are constructed, arriving at the denials that we are made to face in real life. As a result we tend to derive a vicarious satisfaction by identifying ourselves with the heroes. Little room remains for music. At the best it is usually received only half-consciously, not listened to exactly, but absorbed in an associative manner. Where it has the ambition to make independent contributions to the film, i.e. not just to underline the visual events, but also to complete and to interpret them (and it has this ambition more often than one generally assumes), exactly at those points must it make an endeavour to convey its contents through its various associations.

The surest way for this is to work with gesticulatory homophony and with 'reserved materials'. The suspicion remains that perhaps these would have been incorporated in film music anyway even had Mahler's works remained totally ignored.

городу Ленинграду
Симфония № 7
116
I

Arnold Schœnberg

My Opponents

1.
Justified Opposition

(*a*) such that are used to understand, who know what it means to understand; who know what they do not understand;
(*b*) necessary opposite reaction in order to force one to be clear;
(*c*) good musicians of the old school.

2.
Not justified

(*a*) principled opposition against everything new;
(*b*) committed and fixed to aesthetic principles;
(*c*) insensitive and deaf;
(*d*) modern but not ultra-modern compromisers;
(*e*) followers of trends—new trends;
(*f*) marionettes;
(*g*) disciples or hangers on of the successful.

Is a new music necessary?
for whom?
why?

It is necessary and as superfluous as everything else that is new. Certainly, after one has travelled for centuries with the swiftness of horses, one could remain satisfied to do so for centuries longer without needing railways, cars and aeroplanes. So indeed one recognizes the value of the new because of its usefulness without, however, realizing its necessity. Perhaps, the necessity demonstrates itself only after the advantages of the new have become a necessity. Usefulness and necessity in this sense do not exist in Art. That is why we must look for it in ourselves.

But also practically the New in the music is a need, a necessity (in spite of the enjoyment one may have in sinking in the thought of one's predecessors). Try to image a situation, where after a certain point in time, nothing new is created. In such a situation the first question to arise would be, what point in time should one have stopped—in the thirteenth, fourteenth or fifteenth century or in later ones? What would be the things that would then have remained unsaid?

One acknowledges that one could have stopped to create new things after Bach, for example, for that was the start of a new epoch. But could one have satisfied oneself with all that had been created until then? Would not our understanding for Bach be poorer than it is today?[1]

1 Arnold Schönberg, 'Neue Musik—Meine Musik', *Journal of the Arnold Schönberg Institute,* Los Angeles, vol. 1, no. 2, 1977.

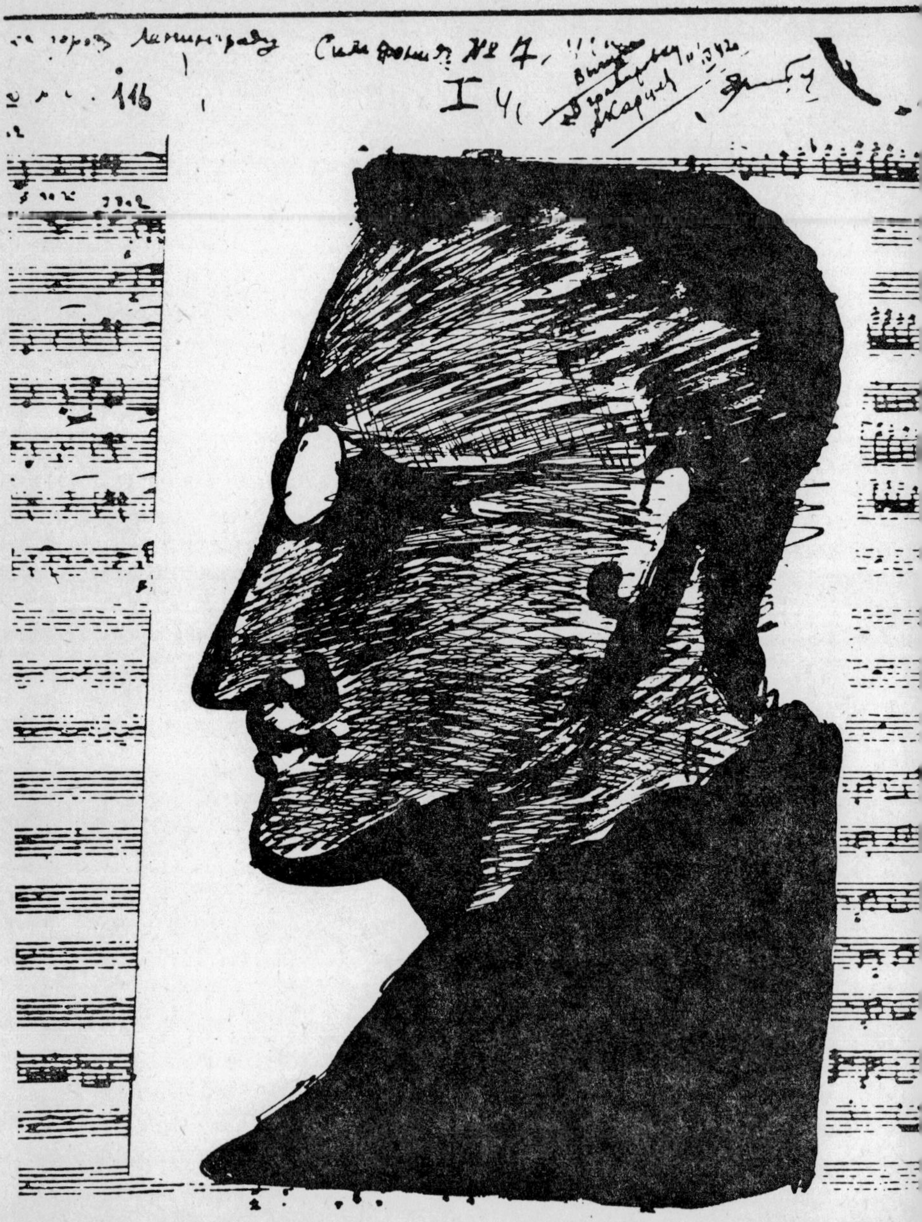
Симфония № 7

Anton von Webern: the man and his music

In his essay 'Anankastic Aspects in Anton Webern's Work', the composer Hubert Stuppner puts forward the opinion that 'in actuality that which occurred with Anton Webern was something one had not expected so early in the twentieth century in the midst of the creative urge of the Decadence. This was the collapse of the Late Romantic, manifested in the catastrophe which could be described as the crisis of a sensitive mimosa-like I or the ego. This was a Self which used numbers and a series to envelop in a silence the shocks and tremors that it knew to be taboo.'

The radical reduction of the musical needs and requirements accompanied by a regression towards primitive structures such as canons, monodies, mirror canons, retrograde motion, inversion, had for Webern a psychological conclusiveness. On one hand these express the *angst* of an heir of early Expressionism. On the other hand these indicate the inner imbalance of the I (the self) which is compensated through the balance of the invented structures and acquires stability through sublimation. In this sense, Webern's sparse tonal gestures have something of the nature of a self, an Ego, that is essentially destroyed adjusting itself, a self which strives for definite forms by substituting musical forms. Thus the historical catastrophe which is reflected in Webern's music is also a catastrophe of the individual. Webern's style is like himself: radical, apodictic, small and emaciated, of scrupulous cleanliness, economical, taciturn, secretly totalitarian. Webern's characteristic structure is characterized by anankastic depression which makes examples by bringing things into contexts everywhere, which aims at the Absolute and seeks to reduce all things to a common denominator. This anankastic nature has a natural sympathy for all examples and instances of the fatal and total context; it is enthused by Goethe's 'Pflanzenlehre', by Strindberg's 'Weltschmerz', by pantheistic philosophical ideas or by a form of religion—the religion of symmetrical dodecaphony: 'That therefore godly things portray themselves in the world in analogies, in parallels'. A shocking fear of separation emerged when Webern's teacher Schönberg declared Webern to be able to stand on his own feet. Webern told Schönberg: 'I plead with you in earnest, please continue to be my guide, please chastise me once again into correction.'

A letter from Webern to Schönberg, discussing Webern's psycho-analytical treatment under Dr Alfred Adler reveals that the creative motivation for the briefest of his pieces had its foundation in a constitutional fear of making decisions: '. . . on the other hand, due to an anxiousness which already began in my childhood, a softness, an overly-great sensibility, I retreat with fear from having to make decisions'. Adler's diagnosis, 'feelings of inferiority', corresponds with the inner disintegration and dejectedness and despondency that Webern complained of himself. The inexorableness with which Webern's serial technique tackles randomness and arbitrariness, has in truth a totalitarian character. There the identification with the early National Socialism with its 'inner purification of the Nation' finds an explanation: 'Inner purification . . . that is Germany today! Created by this man ! ! ! (Hitler) unique—what could have only had this nature as its source, has this unique unequalled (man) for its author-initiator'.

The expression of the *thought* stands at the centre of composing. Webern told the pianist Peter Stadtlen that he had to know how his (Webern's) work has to be *played*, and not, how it is *made*. In his lectures Webern substantiates his concept of music naturally and rationally. The human rationality is the medium through which nature progressively reveals itself in historical process. Tone-systems are nothing other than the 'deposits of overtones', they are not *invented* but found.

The historical roots of Webern's poetics lie in German idealism, especially in the transcendental tonalism. In the transcendental experience the subject forces itself, permeates into Nature; if it bridges the gap between the spiritual and the physical the pure I (self) emerges and commands over the 'intellectual perception', which it transforms into a partner in the production of Nature.

For Webern the difference between 'Science' and 'inspired creation' has melted away. His picture is the series, the idea, which lies at the base of the work.

It was Goethe who had already drawn attention to the conflict between the idea and the experience. For our understanding they are difficult to combine with each other. Research in the natural sciences is limited by space and time. Reason cannot think in a unifying manner about the things that sensual experience delivers to it separately. Carrying this over to Webern's pieces, one can see how the receptive faculties find a lot artificially made; the tendency towards the transcendental is theoretically reconstructable, but often remains abstract and imperative sensually.

городу Ленинграду
Симфония № 7

The Way of Electronic Music

1

Electronic sound is a very recent phenomenon in the history of music. We can look back to its exact date and time of birth. The findings of research into a new kind of sound were presented in the first ever electronic concert in a matinée performance at the Cologne Broadcasting House on 26 May 1953. Electronic Music has been in existence since then.

In fact, what had come into being had long been a dream among musicians. Its origins reach back into the Futurist period, which took Europe by storm as a forceful artistic revolution. The idea of a new sound liberated from any tradition was only a part of the Futurist movement. Its first aim was an elementary revolt against the ballast of the history and traditions of Western art in its entirety. It was an expression of the modern spirit, one which with great pathos championed an altogether new beauty and strove to sacrifice the storehouse of artistic tradition in order to make room for this new sentiment. The signal for the onset of the new spirit was sounded on 12 February 1909, in the famous article by the Italian poet, Filippo Tommaso Marinetti, in the Paris journal *Le Figaro*, and it registered all over Europe. 'We declare,' he wrote, 'that the world's splendours have been enriched by a new beauty, the beauty of speed. A racing car sporting a radiator with fat pipes like serpents with explosive breath . . . a roaring automobile looking as if it were racing along on a pile of grape-shot, is more beautiful than the Nike of Samothrace . . . ' Marinetti wanted to announce the downfall of Western culture, an all-out cultural catastrophe. From its rubble, there was to rise the new, and the artistic youth of Europe who was in one mind about dumping the burden of the old. In Berlin, similar Futurist manifestos were published around 1910 (Horwarth Walden established the journal, *Sturm,* there), as they were in Moscow and Paris. Everywhere the cause was identical with that of the centre of the Futurist movement, Milan; the violent, revolutionary eruption of a new art, the beauty of which was to be the world of the young industrial age. Marinetti enthused about the 'colourful polyphonic surge of industry in motion in the modern metropolis, the steelworks, hung on the clouds by the thread of their smoke, the wide-fronted locomotives pounding over the rails like giant iron horses bridled by long pipes.'

One of the first musicians of the Milan Futurist movement was Luigi Russolo, who wanted to meet the challenge of sound for the new age with bizarre noise-instruments which he called intonarumori, monstrous boxes with horns and levers, handles and buttons which produced whole scales of noises, mostly by mechanical means. In the end, Russolo possessed an entire orchestra of these so-called bruiteurs; he first demonstrated them in Modena in 1913, and then in all the European capitals, where they caused a sensation as curious artefacts of a radical musical avant-grade.

This sound, too, Marinetti had presaged. His manifesto decrees, 'Let music give the masses, the great industrial works, trains, ocean liners, battle cruisers, automobiles and aeroplanes their musical sound, add to the grand and inmost subjects of musical composition the empire of the machine and the victorious dominance of electricity.'

This phrase, the dominance of electricity in music, appears to be almost an early prophecy of electronic music. In fact, one can discern an uninterrupted line of historical development from the stormy beginnings of Futurism to the first emergence of Electronic Music. True, there were many offshoots and variants of this notion of a new world of music. Among these are the many orchestral pieces ranging from the neo-classical to the expressionistic, in which machines and railway trains figure in concert, from Mossolov's 'Iron-works Piece' to Arthus Honegger's famous railway orchestra piece, 'Pacific 231' of 1923.

These apart, the basic idea of a totally innovative musical sound can be found haunting musical thought from the time of Marinetti to the invention of Electronic Music. One of its favourite precepts is the revolt against the strict limitations of classical harmony and the emancipation of noise as a musical sound as valid as any other.

One of the great musicians to follow the Milan movement with sympathy was Ferruccio Busoni. In his famous 'Sketch for a new Aesthetic of Music' of 1910, he paraphrased the idea of a new musical sound in enthusiastic language: 'The child—it floats! Its feet do not touch the earth. It is not subject to gravity. It is almost incorporeal. Its substance is transparent. It is sounding air. It is almost nature herself. It is free.'

A notion such as this, namely that musical sound should be 'emancipated' from the ties of classical rules of composition, that it should develop its own character, this kind of notion is just as influenced by Marinetti's revolution as by the tremendous heightening of sensibility to sound owed to late Romanticism and Impressionism. For the new sound is characterized above all by a property hitherto only subordinate in music, that of colour. At about the same time as Busoni, Arnold Schönberg took up the idea in his 'Theory of Harmony', which was published in 1911, a year after the 'Sketch for a new Aesthetic of Music'. In his theory of harmony, Schönberg considered the possibility of composing with the timbre or colour of a sound and coined the concept of 'tone colour melody'. He posed the question of whether it might be possible to formulate musical thoughts with the colours of sounds, which could then be heard as melodies, just like the melodies one was used to composing with qualities of pitch. Schönberg experimented in composing such tone colour melodies for the instruments of the orchestra, but they proved too rigidly determined and too inflexible in their timbre to produce the gradual changes in tonal colour scale.

To fulfil the old dream of a liberated, floating sound, a new instrument was needed which would be capable of developing the character of a sound in all conceivable textural nuances. It is just this idea, present in essence as early as 1910, that is the birth certificate of Electronic Music.

2

The technical potential had long been there. Even at the beginning of our century, the discovery had been made that sounds could be produced by electrical means in radio or vacuum tubes, then called audions. The first patents were applied for in Paris by the American inventor Lee de Forest in 1915, and spread throughout Europe soon after. But musical instruments incorporating radio tubes were only to occur in the twenties; in Petrograd, the young Leon Theremin constructed his electronic music apparatus, for which Edgar Varèse wrote his composition, 'Equatorial'. Maurice Martenot, a music master and radio telegrapher, demonstrated his 'Ondes Martenot' at the Grand Opéra in Paris; they played a major part in several of Olivier Messiaen's works. In Germany, Friedrich Trautwein constructed his famous Trautenium at the Experimental Broadcast Department of the Musikhochschule in Berlin; Oskar Sala later extended it to a large, multi-textured Mixture Trautonium.

One characteristic was common to all these electric musical instruments: in their function and construction they all resembled traditional instruments—string or keyboard instruments—or they even applied their technical potential to the imitation of classical instrumental colour. The tone colour spectrum of the orchestra had thus been extended by some more or less grotesque colours; but their sound had not by any means brought about that new floating musical quality of which Ferruccio Busoni had dreamt in his 'Sketch'. Basically, the electronic music apparatus had contributed little to change his assertion that 'the development of music founders on our musical instruments'. Meanwhile the idea of a new sound survived the Great War and continued to grow.

At first it was two opposing schools of Electronic Music that rose to eminence in post-war Europe. In Paris, under the influence of the early Futurist noise compositions, there emerged Pierre Schaeffer's 'musique concrètè' which took sounds from the environment as its raw material for recording-tape compositions. The original, diverse sounds are those of machines, trains, but also nature itself; these are subjected to comprehensive technical manipulation such as super-imposition, distortion or echoing, resonance etc., so changing their character that the final product is frequently an abstract sound after all, completely obscuring its origins. French Radio gave the first broadcast of the results of Pierre Schaeffer's work, five études on noise sounds, on 5 October 1948, and entitled it 'Concert de druide'.

The Electronic Music of the Cologne School, which was founded at about the same time at the beginning of the fifties, was much more stringent in its techniques and ideas. It interpreted the thought of a new musical sound as an extremely purist compositional concept. The first 'demonstration samples' of this music were given in May 1953 in a matinée performance as part of the New Music Festival in Cologne, and met with much resonance throughout Europe. The critic, Hans Heinz Stuckenschmidt, then of the *Neue Zeitung*, wrote, 'In the electronic school at Cologne, the machine itself becomes the music's means of performance. As if by a homunculus, the new sound issues from electric monochord and melochord. Sound never yet heard becomes an event, acquires a strange and exciting form; most strikingly so in the three movements of a composition which Robert Beyer calls "Klang im unbegrenzten Raum" or "Sound in infinite space". Here the breakaway from any conception, vocal or instrumental, is complete. The sounds, some of them comparable to the roaring and neighing of animals of steel, seem to mount like spiral bubbles from the mineral world into our consciousness. Intermediate levels of a metamusic have been won, intangible, abstract and yet irresistible in their effect. The dreams of the Bruitists of 1910 have been fulfilled and at the same time left far behind.' Robert Beyer was the technician at the Electronic Studio in Cologne in its early years; together with the composer and journalist, Herbert Eimert, and Bonn scientist, Werner Meyer-Eppler, he used the technical facilities of a broadcasting station to found the first studio which based its work on the systematic analysis of sound. That was in 1951. In the same year as the memorable first concert in Cologne, a young composer named Karlheinz Stockhausen began his work for the Cologne Studio.

Musicography

The musicography offers a selection of recordings available at the Max Mueller Bhavan Library, Calcutta, as a point of reference for the reader who might like to check on or test some of the suggestions made in the course of these lectures. At the same time it could serve a new listener for a guide to introductory or initiatory listening.

MOZART, WOLFGANG A. (1756–1791)

— Complete concertos for violin.—Yehudi Menuhin. Bath Festival Orchestra.

— *Divertimento* No. 14 in B flat major KV 270; *Divertimento* No. 2 in B flat major KV appendix 229; *Divertimento* in C minor KV 388.—The Würzburg Mozart Festival 1976.

— *Don Giovanni*—Opera (Italian).—D. Fischer-Dieskau; E. Flagello; P. Schreier; B. Nilsson; M. Arroyo; M. Talvela; R. Grist; A. Marrotti. National Theater Orchestra, Prague, Karl Böhm.

— *Entführung aus dem Serail* (The Abduction from the Seraglio).—E. Koeth; F. Wunderlich; L. Schaedle; F. Lenz; K. Boehme. Bavarian State Opera and Chorus, E. Jochum.

— *The Marriage of Figaro* (Italian).—G. London; E. Schwarzkopf; S. Jurinac; E. Kunz; I. Seefried. Vienna State Opera Choir. Vienna Philharmonic Orchestra, Herbert von Karajan.

— *Messe* (Mass) KV 139 'Orphanage Mass'. G. Janowitz; F. von Stade; K. Moll; Vienna State Opera Choir. Vienna Philharmonic Orchestra, Karl Böhm.

— *The Magic Flute* (Opera in 2 Acts) in German.—E. Lear; L. Otto; F. Crass; D. Fischer-Dieskau. RIAS Chamber Choir. Berlin Philharmonics, Karl Böhm.

— *The Magic Flute* (Opera in 2 Acts) in German.—H. Güden; W. Berry; W. Lipp; K. Boehme; Ch. Ludwig. Vienna State Opera Choir. Vienna Philharmonics, K. Böhm.

— String Quartet KV 428 No. 16 in E flat major; String Quartet KV 458 No. 17 in B flat major.—Heutling Quartet.

— The Early String Quartets Nos. 1–13; 155–160; 168–173.—Amadeus Quartet.

— *Requiem* KV 626.—E. Mathis; J. Hamari; W. Ochman; K. Ridder-Busch. Vienna State Opera Choir. Vienna Philharmonics, Karl Böhm.

—*Sinfonie Concertante* in E flat major K 364.—I. Stern, violin; P. Zuckerman, viola. English Chamber Orchestra, D. Barenboim.
—*Sinfonie Concertante* in E flat major K 364.—Berlin Philharmonics, Karl Böhm.
—46 Symphonies (collected).—Berlin Philharmonics, Karl Böhm.

BEETHOVEN, LUDWIG VAN (1770–1827)
—Octet in E flat major Op. 103
—The five piano concertos.—W. Kempff; Berlin Philharmonics, F. Leitner, C major Op. 15; B major Op. 19; C minor Op. 37; G major Op. 58; E flat major Op. 73
—*Fidelio* (Opera in 2 Acts).—Altmeyer; Meven; Wohlers; Nimsgern; Jerusalem; Adam.—Radio Chorus, Berlin and Leipzig, Gewandhaus Orchestra, Kurt Masur.
—*Fidelio* (Opera in 2 Acts).—M. Talvela; T. Adam; J. King; G. Jones; F. Crass.—Leipzig Radio Choir; Dresden State Opera Chorus; Dresden State Orchestra. Karl Böhm.
—*Missa Solemnis*.—M. Price; C. Ludwig; W. Ochman; M. Talvela. Vienna State Opera Chorus; Vienna Philharmonics. Karl Böhm.
—Overtures: 'Consecration of the House' Op. 124; *Coriolanus* Op. 62; *The Creatures of Prometheus* Op. 43; *Egmont* Op. 84; *Fidelio* Op. 72 b; 'King Stephen' or 'Hungary's First Benefactor' Op. 117; *Leonore* I–III Op. 132, 72, 72a; *Name Day* Op. 115; *Ruins of Athens* Op. 113.—Berlin Philharmonics, Karajan.
—Complete Piano Sonatas—Claudio Arrau.
—Complete Sonatas for piano and cello.—P. Fournier, cello; A. Schnabel, piano.
—Complete Sonatas for piano and violin including No. 9 Kreuzer in A major Op. 47; 5 Spring in F major Op. 25.—C. Haskill; A. Grumiaux.
—The Early String Quartets Op. 18 Nos. 1–6.—Juillard String Quartet.
—String Quartets Op. 59/1, 2, 3; Op. 74; Op. 95.—Amadeus Quartet.
—The Late String Quartets in E flat major Op. 127; F major Op. 135; B flat major 130; B flat major Op. 133; grand fugue C sharp minor 131; A minor Op. 132.—Amadeus Quartet.
—Symphonies Nos. 1–9. Berlin Philharmonic Orchestra, Karajan.
—32 variations on an original theme in C minor; 6 variations on an original theme in F major Op. 34.—Rudolf Buchbinder, piano
—The Late String Quartets—La Salle Quartet

SCHUBERT, FRANZ (1797–1828)
—*Lieder*: including 'Erlkönig'; 'Jägers Abendled'; 'Wanderers Nachtlied'; 'Du bist die Ruh'.—Dietrich Fischer-Dieskau, baritone; Gerald Moore, piano.

—Lieder Zyklus 'Die Schöne Müllerin', a song cycle by Wilhelm Müller—20 songs. Peter Schreier, tenor; Walter Obertz, piano.

—7 selected songs from 'Die Schöne Müllerin'—Fritz Wunderlich, tenor; Hubert Giesen, piano.

—Music for Rosamunde.—Overture 'The Magic Harp' Ballet music Nos. 1 and 2.—Berlin Philharmonic Orchestra, Karl Böhm.

—Piano Works: 8 sonatas; 'Wanderer Fantasie'; 6 moments musicaux; 11 ecossaises; 16 German dances; 12 German dances; Hungarian melody in B minor; 4 Impromptus; 4 Impromptus; Allegretto in C minor; 3 piano pieces. Alfred Brendel, piano.

—Piano Works: 4 Impromptus Op. 90; sonata in A major; 'Wanderer Fantasie' Impromptu in F minor Op. 142/4; Impromptu in B flat major Op. 142/3. Christoph Eschenbach, piano.

—Piano Works: sonata in B flat major; 'Wanderer Fantasie'; 6 moments musicaux; 4 Impromptus Op. 90; 4 Impromptus Op. 142.—Wilhelm Kempff, piano.

—Quartet movement in C minor; String Quartet in D minor.—Melos Quartet, Stuttgart.

—String Quartet in A minor; String Quartet in G major.—Melos Quartet, Stuttgart.

—Forellen Quintet (The Trout) for piano, violin, viola, cello and bass in A major Op. 114.—Emil Gilels, piano; N. Brainin; P. Schidlof; M. Lovett; R. Zepperitz.

—*Symphony* No. 4 in C minor (Tragic).—Berlin Philharmonic Orchestra, Lorin Maazel.

—*Symphony* No. 8 in B minor (Unfinished).—Berlin Philharmonic Orchestra, Lorin Maazel.

—*Symphony* No. 8 in B minor (Unfinished).—Berlin Philharmonic Orchestra, Karl Böhm.

—*Symphony* No. 9 in C major; *Symphony* No. 5 in B flat major.—Berlin Philharmonic Orchestra, Karl Böhm.

—8 Symphonies.—Berlin Philharmonic Orchestra, Karl Böhm.

SCHUMANN, ROBERT (1810–1856)

—*Carnaval* Op. 9; *Faschingsschwank aus Wien* Op. 26 (Carnival Jest from Vienna).—Arturo Benedetti Michelangeli, piano.

—*Concerto* for piano and orchestra in A minor Op. 54. Wilhelm Bauckhaus, piano. Vienna Philharmonics, Günter Wand.

—*Concerto* for piano and orchestra in A minor Op. 54.—Geza Anda, piano. Berlin Philharmonics, R. Kubelik.

—*Concerto* for cello and orchestra in A minor Op. 129.—M. Rostropowitsch, cello. Moscow State Philharmonic Orchestra.

—*dichterliebe* Op. 48—a song cycle on poems by Heinrich Heine.—16 songs. Harmann Prey, baritone; Karl Engel, piano.

—*Frauenliebe und Leben* Op. 42: 8 songs.—Volksliedchen Op. 51, 2; Widmung Op. 25, 1,—K. Ferrier, alto; J. Newmark, piano.

— *Liederkreis* Op. 39—song cycle on poems by Joseph von Eichendorff. Hermann Prey, baritone; Karl Engel, piano.
— *Symphony* No. 1 in B flat major Op. 38 'Spring Symphony'; *Symphony* No. 2 in C major Op. 61; *Symphony* No. 3 in E flat major Op. 97 'Rhenish Symphony'; *Symphony* No. 4 in D minor Op. 120; Concert* in F major Op. 86 for four horns and orchestra; 'Manfred' Overture Op. 115;—D. Clevenger 1. Horn; R. Oldberg 2. Horn; T. Howell 3. Horn; N. Schweikert 4. Horn. Chicago Symphony Orchestra, Daniel Barenboim.
— Works for Piano Vol. I: 'The Poetic Cycle'—*Carnaval* Op. 9; *Kreisleriana* Op. 16; *Davidsbündler Tänze* Op. 6; *Humoreske* Op. 20; *Papillons* Op. 2; *Waldszenen* Op. 82; *Faschingsschwank aus Wien* Op. 26 (Carnival Jest from Vienna).
— 'The World of Childhood'—Scenes from Childhood Op. 15; Children's Ball Op. 130; Album Leaves Op. 124; Album for the Young Op. 68 (for small and older children); Three Sonatas for the Young Op. 118; 12 pieces for piano—four bands; Ball scenes Op. 109.
— 'The World of Fantasy'—Six Intermezzi Op. 4; Three Romances Op. 28; Four Night pieces Op. 23; Novelette Op. 21; Three Fantasy pieces Op. 111; 8 Fantasy pieces Op. 12; Fantasy in C major Op. 17—Jörg Demus, piano.

LISZT, FRANZ (1811–1886)
— *Concerto* for piano and orchestra No. 1 in E flat major.—M. Argerich, piano. London Symphony Orchestra, C. Abbado.
— *Concerto* for piano No. 1 in E flat major; *Concerto* for piano No. 2 in A major.—Julian von Karolyi, piano. Philharmonic Hungarica, I. Kertesz.
— *A Faust Symphony.*—K. Riegel, tenor; Tanglewood Festival Chorus. Boston Symphony Orchestra, L. Bernstein.
— *Mephisto Waltz* (episode—*Der Tanz in der Dorfschenke*) from Lenaus 'Faust'.—Lazar Berman, piano
— Piano Sonata in B minor.—M. Argerich, piano
— Piano Sonata in B minor.—Lazar Berman, piano
— Symphonic Poems Nos. 3, 4, 2.—No. 3 Les Preludes; No. 4 Orpheus; No. 2 Tasso Lamento e trionto. London Philharmonic Orchestra, B. Haitink.

WAGNER, RICHARD (1813–1883)
— *The Flying Dutchman.*—Gwyneth Jones; Siegfried Wagner; T. Stewart; K. Ridderbusch. Bayreuth Festival Choir and Orchestra, Karl Böhm 1971.

* piece

— *Lohengrin*—Opera in 3 Acts.—Ridderbusch; Kollo; Tomova-Sintow; Nimsgern; Vienna State Opera Choir. Tölz Boys Choir. Berlin Philharmonic Orchestra, Karajan.
— *The Mastersingers of Nuremberg.*—J. Prohaska; M. Müller; M. Lorenz. 1943 Bayreuth Festival Choir and Orchestra, Wilhelm Furtwängler.
— *Parsifal.*—J. King; Gwyneth Jones; Franz Crass; Thomas Stewart; Donald McIntyre; Karl Ridderbusch. Bayreuth Festival Choir and Orchestra 1970, Pierre Boulez.
— *Rienzi Overture.*—Bundesjugendorchestra, Volker Wangenheim.
— *The Ring of the Nibelungs* (The Ring Cycle).—Original recording at the Bayreuth Festival. Bayreuth Festival Orchestra and Chorus, Karl Böhm.
— *Wesendonck Lieder* (Mathilde Wesendonck songs) Christa Ludwig. Gerald Moore, piano.

BRUCKNER, ANTON (1824–1896)
— *Messe* No. 3 in F minor (Mass).—M. Staedler; C. Hellmann; E. Haefliger; K. Borg. Choir and Symphony Orchestra of the Bavarian Radio, E. Jochum.
— 10 Symphonies Nos. 0–9.—Concert-gebouw Orchestra, Amsterdam, Bernhard Haitink.
— *Symphony* No. 8 in C minor.—Berlin Philharmonics, E. Jochum.

MAHLER, GUSTAV (1860–1911)
— *Das Lied von der Erde* (The Song of the Earth).—E. Cavelti; A. Dermota. Vienna Symphony Orchestra, Otto Klemperer.
— *Symphonies* Nos. 1–10.—Bavarian Radio Symphony Orchestra, Rafael Kubelik.

SCHÖNBERG, ARNOLD (1874–1951)
— From 'The Book of the Hanging Gardens': We populate the dusty evening leaves.—Margot Hinnenberg-Lefebre, soprano; H. Roloff, piano.
— *Chamber Symphony* No. 2 Op. 38.—F. Prausnitz. The New Philharmonic Orchestra, London.
— *Concerto* for violin Op. 36; *Concerto* for piano Op. 48.—Z. Zeitlin, violin; A. Brendel, piano. Bavarian Radio Symphony Orchestra, R. Kubelik.
— *Gurra Lieder* (songs).—I. Borkh; K. Engen; H. Toepper; H. Schachtschneider. Bavarian Radio Choir and Symphony Orchestra, Rafael Kubelik.
— *String Sextet* Op. 4.—Brandis/Gelemann, violins; Streheler/Moog, violas; Finke/Nedo, cellos.

— *Verklärte Nacht* (Radiant Night).—English Chamber Orchestra. Daniel Barenboim.

WEBERN, ANTON (1883–1945)

— 6 Bagatelles for String Quartet Op. 9.—La Salle Quartet.

— *Cantata* No. 1 for soprano, choir and Orchestra.—Heather Harper; John Alldis Choir. English Chamber Orchestra, Gary Bertini.

— 6 pieces for orchestra Op. 6.—Nuremberg Philharmonic Orchestra.

— Four pieces for violin and piano Op. 7.—Gerald Jarry, violin; Christian Ivaldi, piano.

— Four pieces for violin and piano Op. 7.—Sophie Hagemann, violin; Ernst Groeschl, piano.

— Three pieces for cello and piano Op. 11.—Michael Tournus, cello; Christian Ivaldi, piano.

— Six pieces for orchestra. — Bundesjugend Orchestra, Volker Wangenheim.

— String Quartet: 5 movements for String Quartet Op. 5; String Quartet Op. 28.—La Salle Quartet.

— *Lieder* (songs).—D. Fischer-Dieskau, baritone; A. Reimann, piano.

— Five songs Op. 3; five songs Op. 4; four songs Op. 12; three songs Op. 25; three songs Op. 23.—Dorothy Dorow, soprano; Ulf Björlin, piano.

— Trio for violin, viola and cello Op. posth.; Trio for violin, viola and cello Op. 20.—Trio à cordes Francaise.

9788170460503

7